Knowlton School of Architecture

Source Books in
Landscape Architecture

2

Ken Smith
Landscape Architect
Urban Projects

Jane Amidon, Series Editor

Princeton Architectural Press, New York

SOURCE BOOKS IN ARCHITECTURE:

Morphosis/Diamond Ranch High School

The Light Construction Reader

Bernard Tschumi/Zénith de Rouen

UN Studio/Erasmus Bridge

Steven Holl/Simmons Hall

Mack Scogin Merrill Elam/Knowlton Hall

SOURCE BOOKS IN LANDSCAPE ARCHITECTURE:

Michael Van Valkenburgh/Allegheny Riverfront Park

Peter Walker and Partners/Nasher Sculpture Center Garden

Published by

Princeton Architectural Press

37 East Seventh Street

New York, New York 10003

For a free catalog of books, call 1.800.722.6657.

Visit our web site at www.papress.com.

© 2006 Princeton Architectural Press

All rights reserved

Printed and bound in China

10 09 08 07 06   5 4 3 2   First edition

The seminars and publications for this series are made possible by the generous support of DeeDee (BSLA 1988, Knowlton School of Architecture) and Herb Glimcher.

Editing: Nicola Bednarek

Design: Jan Haux

Special thanks to: Nettie Aljian, Dorothy Ball, Janet Behning, Megan Carey, Penny (Yuen Pik) Chu, Russell Fernandez, Clare Jacobson, John King, Mark Lamster, Nancy Eklund Later, Linda Lee, Katharine Myers, Lauren Nelson, Molly Rouzie, Jane Sheinman, Scott Tennent, Jennifer Thompson, Paul Wagner, Joseph Weston, and Deb Wood of Princeton Architectural Press —Kevin C. Lippert, publisher

Library of Congress Cataloging-in-Publication Data:

Ken Smith Landscape Architect : urban projects / Jane Amidon ... editor.

　　p. cm. — (Source books in landscape architecture)

　Includes bibliographical references.

　ISBN 1-56898-510-X (alk. paper)

　1. Smith, Ken, 1927—Interviews. 2. Landscape architects—New York (State)—New York—Interviews. 3. Landscape architecture—New York (State)—New York. I. Smith, Ken, 1927– II. Amidon, Jane. III. Ken Smith Landscape Architect (Firm) IV. Series.

　SB470.S57K46 2005

　712'.092—dc22

　　　　　　　　　　　　　　　　2005013766

Contents

Acknowledgments

Ken Smith and his office, Workshop: Ken Smith Landscape Architect (KSLA), proved early to be a provocative and productive subject for the second Source Book in Landscape Architecture. In 2003 the Knowlton School of Architecture was fortunate to host Ken Smith's installation of three Dumpster Gardens on the Ohio State University campus; the project not only caused both joy and consternation within the university audience but indicated the value of provisional landscapes when word was received that the university president had looked down from her window onto Dumpster #2 (planted in scarlet celosia and grey artemisia) and proclaimed the project a success.

Smith's articulate presentation of ideas casts questions toward the making of contemporary urban landscapes, questions whose answering feeds the perpetual freshness of KSLA design. Much appreciation is owed to Ken for his gardens, for his generous time and energies spent in the Glimcher seminars, and for his thoughtful contributions to this publication.

The critical value of this book is much increased by the participation of Peter Reed and Nina Rappaport. Thanks also to the students who joined in the seminar: Jeff Anderson, Michael Denison, Lin Goepfert, Brian Griffith, Tim Hess, Kris Lucius, Jill McKain, Gabriela Patocchi, Cheryl Somerfeldt, and especially Jason Brabbs, for his videography. Matt Ogborn was a champion transcriber.

The Source Books in Landscape Architecture would not be possible without the generous patronage of DeeDee and Herb Glimcher and the support of many at the Knowlton School of Architecture. Specifically, the encouragement of Director Robert Livesey is essential to the program. I am thankful for advice offered by colleagues and for the logistical help of Ken Smith's studio, in particular Senior Associate Elizabeth Asawa. Priscilla McGeehon shared insightful comments into the work of Ken Smith. Finally, the editorial guidance of Nicola Bednarek and Kevin Lippert at Princeton Architectural Press is very much appreciated.

Source Books in Landscape Architecture

Source Books in Landscape Architecture provide concise investigations into contemporary designed landscapes by looking behind the curtain and beyond the script to trace intentionality and results. One goal is to offer unvarnished stories of place-making. A second goal is to catch emerging and established designers as facets of their process mature from tentative trial into definitive technique.

Each Source Book presents one project or group of related works that are significant to the practice and study of landscape architecture today. It is our hope that readers gain a sense of the project from start to finish, including crucial early concepts that persist into built form as well as the ideas and methods that are shed along the way. Design process, site dynamics, materials research, and team roles are explored in dialogue format and documented in photographs, drawings, diagrams, and models. Each Source Book is introduced with a project data and chronology section and concludes with an essay by an invited critic.

This series was conceived by Robert Livesey at the Austin E. Knowlton School of Architecture and parallels the Source Books in Architecture. Each monograph is a synthesis of a single Glimcher Distinguished Visiting Professorship. Structured as a series of discussion-based seminars to promote critical inquiry into contemporary designed landscapes, the Glimcher professorships give students direct, sustained access to leading voices in practice. Students who participate in the seminars play an instrumental role in contributing to discussions, transcribing recorded material, and editing content for the Source Books. The seminars and Source Books are made possible by a fund established by DeeDee and Herb Glimcher.

Foreword

I had good news and bad news for Ken Smith when I called him in 2002. The Museum of Modern Art (MoMA) wanted to commission a beautiful and imaginative landscape atop the roof of its new gallery building in midtown Manhattan designed by Yoshio Taniguchi. That was the good news. But the project came with a long list of restrictions that could hardly be attractive to a landscape architect: live plants were strongly discouraged; the need for water was to be minimized or eliminated altogether; the height of the landscape could not exceed about three feet; the acceptable roof load was minimal; black and white stones (roof ballast) had already been purchased and ideally should be incorporated in the new design; and the budget was slim. Besides, there was no public access to the roof garden. In fact, museum-goers would never see the roof; only people in the surrounding buildings, notably residents of the adjacent Museum Tower condominium, would enjoy the view from above. This was a work to be looked at, not walked through. After explaining this litany of restrictions, there was a pause on the phone, followed by Smith's somewhat cautious reply, "Well, I'll see what I can do."

Smith's past projects, such as his Glowing Topiary Garden and the P.S. 19 schoolyard, suggested that he was an ideal candidate to take on the museum's roof garden. His work demonstrated a remarkable ability to confront the common reality of many urban sites—hardscapes and low budgets—and produce unconventional designs that are hybrids between landscape architecture and environmental art. His approach stretches the conventional definition of landscape in response to a specific program that itself suggests a focus on aesthetic or practical issues more than ecological processes. Smith's ideas are bold, evocative, and sometimes humorous, and in some respects share a sensibility with other designers, particularly Martha Schwartz, with whom Smith previously worked.

In his first proposal for the roof garden, Smith threw caution to the wind. Fields of ordinary colorful pinwheel daisies are "planted" in a grid of fluorescent green PVC pipe—Andy Warhol meets John Waters meets Kmart. The image of six thousand whirling daisies arranged in great washes of color was humorous, irreverent, and potentially very beautiful, especially when viewed from an optimal distance. The neighboring residents, however, were not convinced that kitsch would be elevated to the status of art.

Some weeks later Smith submitted a new proposal, which explored ideas of camouflage and concealment using real and plastic stones, plastic shrubs and grass, crushed glass, and brick. These elements could be arranged in several ways. Schemes varied from a rectilinear geometry that echoes the Miesian grid of Philip Johnson's Abby Aldrich Rockefeller Sculpture Garden (1953) several stories below to an organic free-form that imitates camouflage patterns and recalls the idiosyncratic designs of the renowned Brazilian landscape architect Roberto Burle-Marx, such as his roof garden for the Ministry of Education building in Rio de Janeiro (1936–38). The camouflage garden prevailed—beautiful in its own right, and standing in contrast to the controlled orthogonal geometry of Johnson's garden and Taniguchi's architecture. Several blocks away at Times Square, the roof of the U.S. Armed Forces Recruiting Station, a small one-story pavilion designed by Architectural Research Office (1998), is painted in military camouflage pattern. Here, the roof decoration does not conceal the structure but is tantamount to a billboard advertising the activities within the building. Smith's roof garden neither conceals nor is intended to evoke military associations. But because of its unconventionality and bold contrast with the surrounding environment, it too calls attention to the institution within, hopefully to the delight and curiosity of those who see it.

Rather than cover its roof in ordinary stone ballast, the museum seized an opportunity for a more creative solution. As such, the roof garden project is not unlike MoMA's exhibition programs that present emerging talent and foster experimentation. The museum's project series, begun in 1971, was conceived as a forum for new artists and has been central to the role of contemporary art at MoMA. Similarly, the Young Architects Program, which takes place every summer in P.S. 1's courtyard and is now in its fifth year, has resulted in astonishingly innovative temporary structures. MoMA's Sculpture Garden has also been the setting for architectural projects, most recently, Shigeru Ban's first work in the United States, Paper Arch (2000), a monumental lattice roof made of paper tubes.

Smith's roof garden, although located outside the parameters of a public gallery, is intended to be no less a compelling work. And as evidenced by the three projects presented in this monograph, finding solutions outside conventional parameters is just where Ken Smith's work wants to be.

Peter Reed
Curator, The Museum of Modern Art

The Museum of Modern Art, Roof Garden

CLIENT:

The Museum of Modern Art

DATA:

North roof: 10,200 square feet
South roof: 7,200 square feet

Material palette:
560 artificial boxwood, 26 inches height
147 sheets Duragrate molded fiberglass grating, 1 inch thick, 1/12 inch square mesh
475 grey PVC pipe segments and 1,120 grey PVC flange pieces for boxwood assembly
2,425 linear feet CNC-cut foam headers, painted Benjamin Moore Hillsboro beige
124 artificial rocks, black
61 artificial rocks, white
306 one-pound bags recycled tumbled glass aggregate, #2 clear
705 fifty-pound bags white marble chips, 2-inch diameter
235 forty-pound bags recycled black rubber mulch, 1-inch chips

26 April 2002

On invitation by MoMA, Ken Smith submits materials for unspecified purpose.

Early November 2002

Smith meets with museum staff and curators to discuss parameters of the roof project.

December 2002

Smith develops Photoshop studies for two alternate concepts that explore flowers as subject matter and writes description of the Field Daisies. A model is made of the assembly proposal and a mock-up is fabricated on the MoMA rooftop. A Quicktime video is made and the ideas are presented to MoMA curators.

27 January 2003

Project is presented to Museum Tower condominium board for approval. At end of the month word is received that the Field Daisies concept is rejected by the condominium board. Meetings with Peter Reed and other MoMA staff ensue to discuss next steps.

Summer 2003

Smith develops camouflage concepts. Materials and detailing research mock-ups are done in KSLA studio.

11 September 2003

Four camouflage design concepts are presented to MoMA curators and staff. "Imitation" and "Deception" are selected for presentation to condominium board. A mock-up is placed on the MoMA roof in advance.

November 2003

The design is approved and Deception becomes the primary scheme. Materials, detailing, and pricing research proceed with design development.

January 2004

Chalk-line mock-up is done on roof to test out the horizontal geometry of the scheme at full size. Initial bids reveal that the project is substantially over budget. Value engineering begins. By June the project is re-bid for a third time and a final cost estimate is accepted in September.

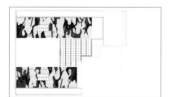

Data and Chronology

February–March 2004
Camouflage schemes exhibited at Harvard University Graduate School of Design.

September–October 2004
KSLA staff visits CNC shop to view mock up; digital files for CNC-cut foam headers and fiberglass grating are issued with final construction documents.

11 November 2004
New York Times columnist Anne Raver writes an advance review of the MoMA roof garden design: "A Rooftop Garden With Synthetic Green."

3 January 2005
Construction commences.

22 February 2005
Construction reaches point of substantial completion with completed punch list. The previous day the *New York Post* publishes a photo of the garden entitled "It's Art-ificial." Three days later Peter Reed's MoMA show "Groundswell, Constructing the Contemporary Landscape" opens. The rooftop garden is represented in the exhibition but public access is not (and never will be) allowed.

April–May 2005
Peter Mauss of Esto photographs the project.

East River Ferry Landings

CLIENT:
New York City Economic Development Corporation
New York City Department of Transportation
New York City Department of Parks and Recreation

DATA:
Total project coverage: 1.5 acres divided into four sites
Thirty-fourth Street site: .78 acres with approximately 2,000 square feet of marsh planters
Size of marsh planters: 20 feet by 81 feet in nine modules

Marsh planter elements:
1 pump
1 saltwater irrigation channel
9 saltwater scuppers
9 freshwater pop-up spray irrigation systems
48 iva frutescens (marsh elder or high tide bush)
864 spartina alternifolia (smooth cord grass)

Fall 2000
Smith is notified that his office has been placed on a shortlist of design consultants for a new ferry landing project on the East River. KSLA teams up with Kennedy & Violich Architecture in a competition against four other design teams, and is selected for the commission.

January–June 2001
Smith prepares plans for temporary landing at East Sixty-seventh Street with Jersey barriers, crib wall planters, and taxodium bosque planting.

October 2002
Project submitted to New York City Fine Art Commission for project approval.

December 2003
Approval received.

March 2004
50% construction documents delivered. Following the initial cost estimate, value engineering begins.

October 2004
100% construction documents delivered.

August 2001
KSLA presents scale model and Smith's Photoshop diagrams for new marsh planter box scheme. Soon after, Smith develops the folded geometry parti in a photomontage.

Post-September 11, 2001
Following the terrorist attacks on the World Trade Center the project goes on hold for six months.

April 2005
The project is out for final bids. The marsh planters are listed as an "Add Alternate" for bidding.

P.S. 19

CLIENT:
The Robin Hood Foundation

DATA:
Site: 32,800 square feet (excluding building footprints)

Site components:
15 custom modified dumpsters, 2 cubic yards
1,974 square feet nylon scrim at 246 feet, 9 inches by 8 feet
7,600 square feet Learning Garden

Learning Garden elements:
960 square feet wood chip path
16 logs
20 types of perennials and annuals, 4,113 total planted
14 types of shrubs, 106 total planted
5 types of trees, 6 total planted

May 2002
Smith receives call from Robin Hood Foundation about a possible schoolyard project in Queens.

15 June 2002
Smith makes first site visit to see the project.

16 June 2002
Smith presents booklet of Photoshop "before and after" imagery illustrating five low-cost prototype schoolyard improvements to the project manager at the Robin Hood Foundation. Receives a call within hours: "Client loves it."

July–October 2002
Design development and construction drawings are prepared.

Early April 2003
Smith supervises soil placement, berm layout, and scrim installation. KSLA completes final berm grading plans and works with the New York Restoration Project to prepare the site and stake out the bird and butterfly garden.

January–February 2003
Planting plans for bird and butterfly garden are prepared.

March 2003
Smith selects specimen logs for the garden.

29 March 2003
Mock-up of dumpster planter is created in West Babylon, New York.

Late April 2003
Logs and plants are delivered to the site. On Earth Day volunteers from the Timberland Corporation do initial plantings. All KSLA staff are on site to supervise the volunteer efforts throughout the planting area. Additional plantings are installed through May.

Summer 2003
Paul Warchol photographs the site.

August–September 2004
Metropolis magazine publishes the project: "Garden Spot."

October 2004
Project receives an ASLA Merit Award.

November 2002
Painted graphics element of project is completed and Albert Večerka of ESTO photographs the site.

Conversations with Ken Smith

Compiled and edited by Jane Amidon

Jane Amidon: **What's important now in your work and how does this relate to the development of your practice?**

Ken Smith: There are several threads that I think are very important. First, if you want to practice landscape architecture seriously, you must have a commitment to public space. You should also be committed to environmentalism, and although the latter is not immediately obvious in most of my projects, it's implicit in my thinking about landscape. And finally, you must have a commitment to history, a respect for history, which I hope is also implicit in my work. These three social agendas, if you will, are crucial to a critical practice. Because my designs are often based on minimalism, icons, and irony, I feel it's even more essential not to gloss over the seriousness of my practice and the non-ironic aspects that underpin it. A sensitivity for public space, environmentalism, and commitment to history are

the underlying qualities of my work that allow its other aspects—the formal qualities and the commentary on contemporary culture—to come to bear on the projects, whether they are small gardens or urban spaces or complex larger sites such as rehabilitating a landfill. Obviously, you can't design a landfill on the basis of irony—you must deal with those other issues of ecology and social space and history.

JA: **What are the roots of the minimalist and iconic tendencies in your work as well as the other threads you mention? Does a multiplicity of readings obscure a critical stance as much as enrich it?**

KS: I'm comfortable with an open interpretation of my projects. I like that there's a certain inherent abstractness at the center of a project's content so the understanding of it can shift and it can have multiple meanings. I think that's what makes

Hiriya Landfill Park competition (Ken Smith in
collaboration with Mierle Ukeles; Julie Bargmann,
D.I.R.T. Studio; and Laura Starr, Saratoga Associates),
Tel Aviv, 2004

landscape work over time. Take Central Park, for
example. My reading of the park is that once you
strip away the well-worn narrative of mitigating
the urban ills, at the core it's basically abstract
content—a great emptiness at the heart of the city.
Central Park has survived because people can project on it new and evolving meaning—each generation can find what it needs, and the park's content
can shift with the times and with cultural changes.
This is also true of Japanese gardens such as
Ryoan-Ji in Kyoto, or places like Walter De Maria's
Lightning Field, where the level of abstractness
allows an openness of interpretation and meaning.

In my thinking about landscape I learned
from both Peter Walker's minimalism and Martha
Schwartz's pop approach. I was hired by Martha
right out of graduate school at Harvard, where I
was a student of Peter Walker. Pete and Martha
were partners at the time, and I was basically
Martha's entire staff at first while Pete had a substantial amount of projects and a solid staff and

design team. Martha's side of the office was often
referred to as the "play pen", but there was a seri-
ous exchange of ideas between both sides of the
office, and I learned tremendously from both Pete
and Martha. Understanding their different strategies—Martha's in-your-face approach and Pete's
more subtle but calculated design strategies—pro-
vided me with a good set of book ends for my
own practice. The importance of history became
clear to me while working in their office, because
their work was rooted in cultural precedents, in
understanding that we are part of a continuum
and that there is a deep well of design history and
traditions to draw upon in innovating contemporary design.

The emphasis of their office was on reinvigo-
rating the art of landscape architecture. When
I moved to New York City to open my own office,
I found it necessary to emphasize public space
and the social aspects of design as part of the art
of my practice. And increasingly, ecology and

Hiriya Landfill Park competiton, Tel Aviv, 2004

TOP: Montage of dumpster planters, study
CENTER: Dumpster Gardens #3, Ohio State University,
May–July 2003
BOTTOM: Dumpster Gardens, Queens Plaza competition,
New York, 2001

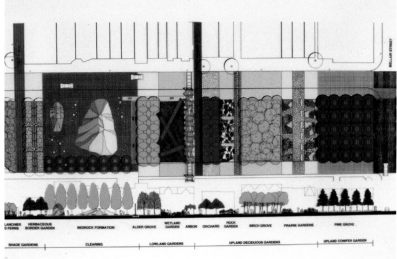

Village of Yorkville Park, Toronto, Canada, 1992–94

environmentalism are growing as an artistic instrument in my design work. Environmentalism is probably something that is generational. It has a stronger current today than twenty years ago. By the 1980s, the profession had set up a dichotomy between environmental planning and form- or space-driven design. At some point you realize that this is a ridiculous and counterproductive dichotomy and that it's much more substantive to combine all elements—to do work that's environmentally sensitive and artistically strong in terms of its medium as well as socially responsible in its use of public space and sustainability.

JA: **But can you really have it all, Ken?**

KS: I don't know. I'm finding out.

JA: **How does a project get born in your office— what's the pattern of interaction between you, clients, your studio team?**

KS: I tend to develop ideas in the office that are then explored in various projects in different ways under different circumstances. The lineage of certain ideas can be traced from project to project. For example, a few years ago I became interested in the idea of containers. I proposed using trash and construction dumpsters in a way similar to conventional flower boxes but larger in size and scope; this developed into the container concepts at P.S. 19, Queens Plaza, and in the installation of dumpster gardens at the Ohio State University. The marsh planters in the East River project are a variation on this interest in the container, as is the collection box idea I used at Yorkville Park.

Another idea deals with the concept of vertical green—the notion that landscape can occupy or co-habit with urban infrastructure in a vertical or structured way. This goes back to the question of how you find space to make landscape in highly built urban areas. I experimented with this idea at the Time Warner Center at Columbus Circle, where

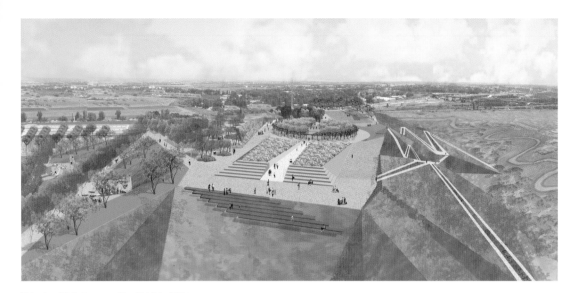

Hiriya Landfill Park competition, Tel Aviv, 2004

I designed a folded stainless-steel "topiary wall" that is planted to create a vertical landscape, and at a museum in Queens where I proposed a topiary curtain. At the museum project, photographing the site gave me the idea of creating a kind of theatrical curtain along one edge with fluid folds that could be planted with vines. In another current project also in Queens I have proposed a series of large billboard structures for the top of several low-rise buildings that would be planted with vines, a kind of green signage if you will. Related to the idea of vertical green is my current interest in pleats, a kind of folding that articulates form. One of the first projects of this type is a small urban courtyard in Manhattan, which is going to have a folded-form topiary screen constructed of an armature with stainless-steel mesh panels and vines. I used pleats in the Hiriya landfill project in Tel Aviv, and the East River Ferry Landings project also has a folding form—origami folding in this case—as does the Time Warner project.

Another major thread in my work is appropriation and found objects. The dumpsters are certainly a manifestation of this. Part of this is also my interest in using contemporary materials that are intended for other uses. The Aluminum Garden, where I used factory grating, structural marine channels, and heavy construction timber is an example. My interest in found objects and their transformation is explored in the Hotel Eden installation for *Nest* magazine and in the MoMA roof garden. The roof garden takes this aspect of appropriation to a new level of simulation.

In terms of how we work as a studio, I tend to start out with an initial idea that I want to explore artistically and to which the project is suited. Typically I think before I begin to draw. I like using Photoshop in early design stages as a sketching tool to make montages and diagrams of initial concepts. I mostly do these studies myself, because they allow me to develop ideas and a lineage of thought. I often use a combination of

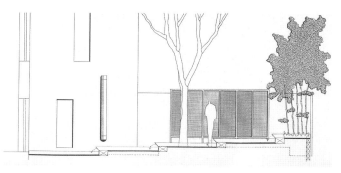

TOP left: Aluminum Garden, New York City, 1999

TOP right: Aluminum Garden

CENTER: Hotel Eden, artificial garden installation for *Nest* magazine, 2000

BOTTOM: The Museum of Modern Art, New York City, Roof Garden, 2003–05

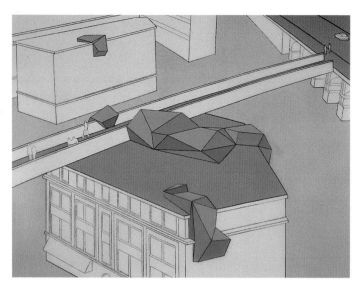

Mutant Gardens, Lausanne, Switzerland, 1999

Google downloads and my own image and reference collection in generating concept images. It's pretty common for me to start out with these Photoshop sketches before the office does any kind of CAD work. Often I go from these studies directly to model and then finally to CAD production. I'm a committed model builder. Even though I don't usually have the luxury of building complete models myself any more, I still like to work with small study models to help me understand the form of something I'm thinking about, and models are constructed throughout the design process—eventually even at full size to test out form and scale of features I am prototyping.

JA: **What's your take on systematic randomness?**

KS: I'm interested in process and how process can be a generator of form. I'm a fan of minimalist music, for example, where process and structure are used to create an experiential art form. In my own work, I'm interested in developing a kind of randomness that is rooted in geometry. For an interior wall in the new café at the Cornerstone Garden Festival in Sonoma, I came up with the idea of "wallflowers"—artificial flowers that are pinned to the wall according to an invisible grid. It's a bit of a Sol Lewitt notion that the flowers can occupy the center of the grid, one of four sides, or one of four corners—there are nine possible positions and a limited range of flower choices. I clipped the images of flowers from another project I had in my computer to test out the grid palette, pulling a flower, picking an unused position, and applying it until the field was exhausted, then starting the process over again and again until the entire wall was complete. In the final installation, the grid is gone but you can sense it, when you look at the random patterning. It's like when you touch poison ivy and get these lines of welts on your skin. You can read the lines as geometric forms but behind the overt geometry there is this

Glowing Topiary Garden (Ken Smith in collaboration with Jim Conti), New York City, 1997

other dynamic—the pattern exists between geometry and that other force. Your eye wants to recognize an order but you can't quite pin it down.

JA: **You initially gained publicity in design circles for your smaller-scale provisional installations such as the Glowing Topiary Garden, Mutant Gardens, or the Fifth Avenue Chandelier proposal. In discussions in 1990, you stressed the subversive nature of temporary work as a primary interest. Today you are working on large-scale, "permanent" landscapes, and you list public space, history, and environmentalism as mandates for success. Do small, temporary works still matter in your practice?**

KS: I've always thought of the provisional projects as a kind of research and development tool. I like to compare this to the workings of a fashion house such as Christian Dior or Jean Paul Gaultier. A fashion house consists of a whole range of

products—with the couture line being the most important line of production artistically speaking. But the fashion house also has ready-to-wear and bridge lines, perfumes and accessories, and other products that extend the ideas developed for the couture line in different but still artistically significant directions. Early in my office's history, I used to talk about this, about having different kinds of product lines: there are the art installations, the public projects, and the residential work. I was never interested in establishing the kind of office that focuses only on one singular thing. Instead I wanted to develop a general practice that allows a wide range of work.

At first, it was difficult to get larger public projects because nobody was going to trust somebody with little or no experience in this area. But now I'm at a point where I have the opportunity to do more large-scale work. In my practice, there's a link between strategy and concept, and materiality and detail. Missing that link is one of the fundamental problems with a lot of landscape architecture practices: there are people who do only theoretical and conceptual work and never get anything built, and there are people who are really good at building and detailing but don't have any ideas. And then there are the critical practices and a few good firms in the country that are engaged at both levels. My ambition is to create work that is conceptually grounded and materially rigorous with a strong connection between idea and design form and material resolution. I think that the experimentation with and risk taking involved with the temporary or provisional projects is essential in testing and developing ideas that can come to bear in the execution of larger and more complex built projects.

JA: **The "Groundswell" show at MoMA opened in February of 2005. It documents the profession's current occupation with, in curator Peter Reed's words, "new urban landscapes" of the post-industrial era that "did not exist as public space half a generation ago." In the same way that we look back to Elizabeth Kassler's 1964 MoMA publication *Modern Gardens and the Landscape* as a signal that modernism had coalesced into a dominant postwar paradigm, what does an exhibition such as "Groundswell" say to you as a landscape architect, and how will your work be positioned in the coming decades of post-productive sites?**

KS: The "Groundswell" exhibition is a kind of summary of the dominant ideas to emerge in landscape architecture at the end of the twentieth century and the beginning of this new century. It marks a transition in the production of landscape space from modern to postmodern. It is really no longer feasible—economically, socially, or environmentally—to continue with the exploitation of raw space that typified a lot of the modern-era production. Today the most interesting and responsible work is occurring in the margins of leftover and reclaimed space. This includes working within the constraints of existing urban fabric, recovering defunct manufacturing areas, derelict waterfronts, and marginal urban fringe areas; creating new public uses in the subsidiary spaces that occur alongside infrastructure; rethinking small leftover urban spaces for new social uses; and reclaiming environmentally damaged spaces such as brownfields. The difficulty of working with these types of spaces lies in creating new design approaches that respond to new programmatic demands, challenging environmental conditions, and the realities of contemporary life. I think the work in the MoMA show is a response to this changing field of landscape design. In my own work I have experimented with new design methodologies. I am as interested in inductive "bottom-up" design approaches that favor context and opportunistic tactics as I am in larger strategic "top-down" approaches that favor systems and broad conceptual ideas. I think the same is true for a whole younger generation of designers. I like to work a problem conceptually from both ends to see where the solution finds resolution in the middle.

The Museum of Modern Art, Roof Garden

New York, New York

In 2002 MoMA curator Peter Reed asked Ken Smith to propose an "imaginative" roofscape installation for the new gallery addition by architect Yoshio Taniguchi. Never to be accessible to the general public, the 17,400 square-foot garden, sitting six floors above street level, was destined to function more as one of the museum's collected works of modern and contemporary art than as an inhabitable landscape. Numerous design considerations included weight restrictions, zero tolerance for irrigation, no elements above three feet in height, and a low budget. Smith's first proposal was disallowed, sending the designer back to the drawing board to devise a final scheme of a contextually alert, patterned surface condition.

JA: **Your first scheme for the MoMA rooftop was a success on the lecture circuit and in its eventual installation at the Cornerstone Garden Festival in Sonoma, California. But it was rejected by MoMA's residential neighbors, who had right of refusal and indeed are the primary audience for the rooftop site. What did you learn from the first scheme's failure, and how did that guide your ideas for the second scheme?**

KS: The first scheme that I came up with was a grid of spinning daisies, an optical field of plastic flowers that reacted to wind movement. The idea was maybe too obvious. I think the Museum Tower's residential co-op board didn't like its overt nature. So for the next proposal I thought that a study of camouflage would be a good starting point for getting an interesting scheme under the radar, as it were.

JA: **Is it problematic if the design succeeds to the point that it's rendered invisible, i.e., if a viewer misses the point? Does the term camouflage need to be used explicitly in relation to the project?**

The flower motif in modern art

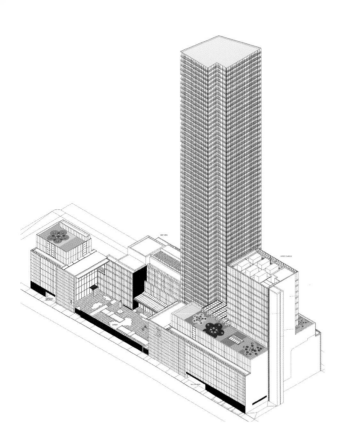

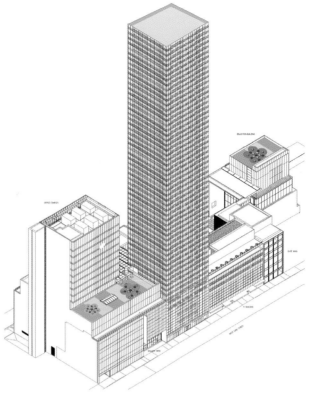

An alternative initial design scheme featured the daisy flower as an icon.

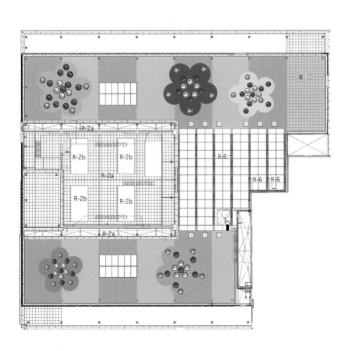

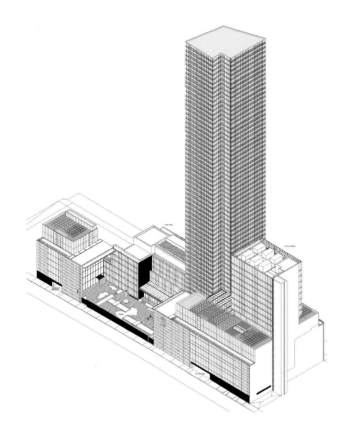

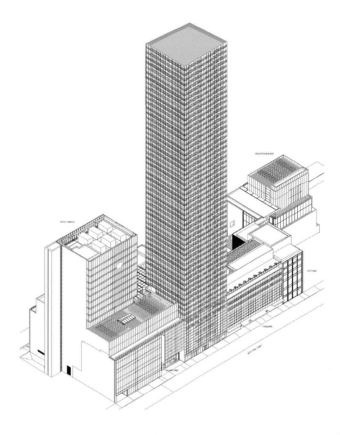

Smith's first, rejected design scheme for the roof garden was based on a field of spinning lawn flowers.

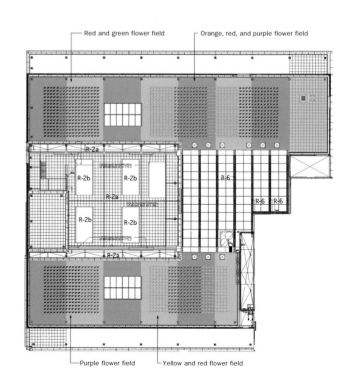

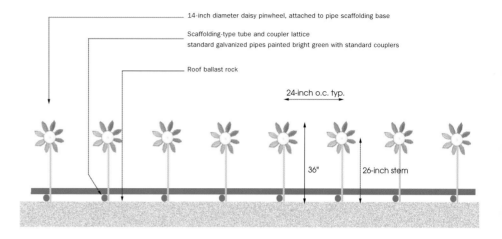

14-inch diameter daisy pinwheel, attached to pipe scaffolding base

Scaffolding-type tube and coupler lattice
standard galvanized pipes painted bright green with standard couplers

Roof ballast rock

24-inch o.c. typ.

36"

26-inch stem

KS: I think it's hardly invisible. When I presented the project for approval, I didn't hammer the point home, I didn't start off by saying, "this is about camouflage," which would actually have been quite counterproductive. I talked about the garden in different terms, but my presentation acknowledged what it was about and how it was operating. The design is about simulation. In fact, creating a landscape garden on a rooftop is inherently an act of simulation. I am very interested in how camouflage simulates landscape, and in this garden the landscape simulates camouflage simulating landscape.

There is a whole series of different camouflage strategies that were developed at a critical moment of the late 1930s and early 1940s—coinciding with World War II. People then were very interested in the notion of camouflage—scientists as well as designers and artists. In the architecture magazines of the time there was a critical discussion about the role of camouflage in defense. I remember that

as a student I read the old *Pencil Points* articles by Dan Kiley, James Rose, and Garrett Eckbo. In the same bound volume of the magazine there was an article on the art and theory and techniques of camouflage. It was geared toward architects and talked about how you could camouflage buildings for reasons of national security. I always thought that camouflage was an interesting quality and did my first camouflage studies during the late 1980s. It was an idea that I had played with but had never gotten to the point of executing.

JA: **Does the making of a constructed landscape always imply the artifice of simulation? Some would say that all acts of design camouflage truth while others say it's a bringing forth, an agent of clarification and amplification.**

KS: The history of garden design is filled with examples of simulation and camouflage. Central Park, for example, is a large-scale garden that artistically simulates visual and spatial aspects of an idealized pre-industrial arcadia and disguises a large territory of the Manhattan grid with imitated nature. Contemporary landscape design often deals with the fundamental issue of ameliorating or covering up the impacts of the constructed environment. Practitioners refer to this as "remediation," "shrubbing it up," "contextualization," or simply "naturalizing." This practice of landscaping as camouflage is a common but critically unrecognized aspect of simulation in the landscape architecture profession.

Four basic camouflage strategies were identified by *Architect and Engineer* magazine in 1942: imitation, deception, decoy, and confusion. Imitation camouflage is the most common and widely used technique. It is the blending in with surrounding territory so that the subject is indistinguishable from its setting. Whether it is in the country or city, desert or forest, summer or winter, the subject appears to be part of the surrounding landscape.

Deception camouflage is a method that does not attempt to completely hide the subject but to change its appearance enough that it resembles something of a different or innocuous nature. The principle is employed to deceive the bombardier who is looking for a powerhouse and finds only an "apartment house" with awnings and shrubs. Decoy camouflage is achieved through the construction of dummy objects in conjunction with the concealment of real ones so that enemy bombers will be attracted to false targets. Confusion is the least used camouflage procedure and consists of concealing the subject by impairing vision or judgment by presenting a multiplicity of potential or illogical targets that confuse accurate determination.

In contemporary urban life, "camouflage" is ironically used to both blend in and stand out. The MoMA project takes the art of camouflage and the artifice of simulation a step further by using the simulation itself as a source for design speculation. One might think of this as the simulation of a simulation, or using imitated nature to generate a new nature.

Roof gardens are inherently artificial environments. They have limitations of weight loading, there are issues of how to anchor elements and protect the waterproof membrane, as well as environmental issues of wind, access to light, and generally harsh conditions for living plants, including limited maintenance and care. Simultaneously, the design of these spaces is often driven by the desire to impose the imagery of imitated nature onto these built constructions.

JA: **Describe your four design proposals for the rooftop according to the categories of imitation, deception, decoy, and confusion.**

KS: The most common camouflage strategy is imitation. If you have a building sitting in the middle of the woods, you imitate the woods to blend in. For a building in midtown Manhattan, imitation means

employing rectilinear forms that have the shape of skylights, vents, or elevator shafts—the sort of platforms you find on the top of buildings that blend into the urban landscape. So our first scheme was very rectilinear—a kind of Peter Walker scheme.

The second strategy is based on deception, in this case making the rooftop look like something it isn't, as opposed to blending in. I used curvilinear forms to imitate Central Park, which is just a few blocks north of the building. I applied the iconic camouflage pattern you find in military clothing to make reference to Olmsted's landscaping.

Decoy is the third approach, the one where you basically throw the viewer off track by building a dummy target. For that scheme I created a folded landscape that was neither building nor nature—it was just a false thing up there, a red herring.

The fourth strategy was confusion. In the magazine article this approach was described as building fires or something else to obscure the vision of the pilots. I interpreted it as just doing

In the late 1930s and early 1940s, the role of camouflage in defense was discussed in various architecture magazines.

"CAMOUFLAGE—aesthetics and technique,"
Architectural Review vol. 96 (September 1944)

"Industrial Plant Protection,"
Architectural Forum vol. 77 (August 1942)

"Industrial Plant Protection,"
Architectural Forum vol. 77 (August 1942)

"The Camoufleur and His Craft,"
The Builder vol. 157 (October 1939)

Camouflage design concept alternatives for the roof garden

Imitation

Deception

Decoy

Confusion

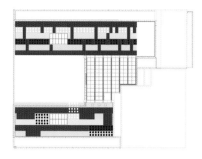

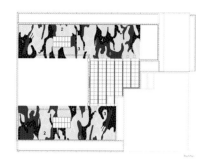

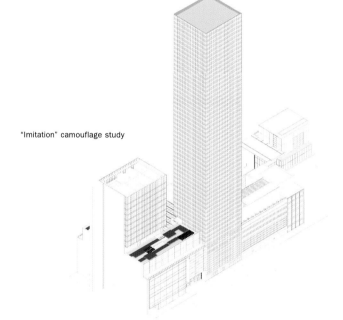

"Imitation" camouflage study

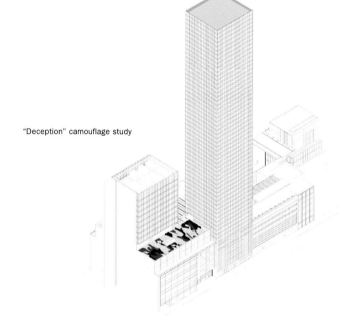

"Deception" camouflage study

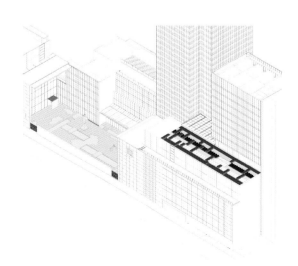

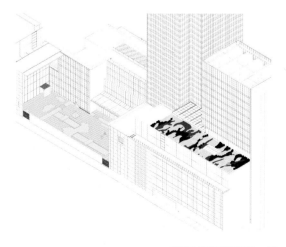

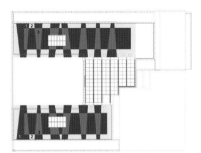

1) Black pebbles
2) White pebbles
3) Plants

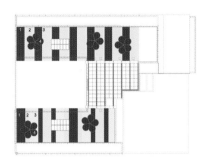

1) Black pebbles
2) White pebbles
3) Crushed glass
4) Plants

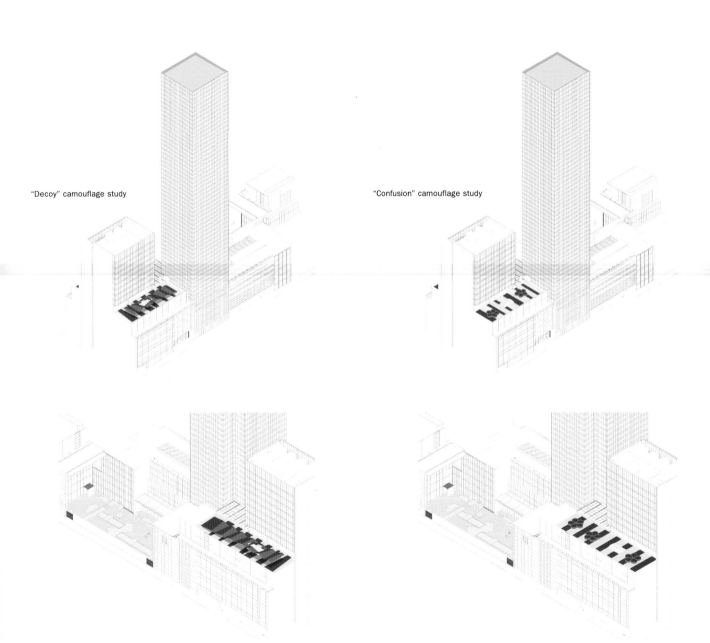

"Decoy" camouflage study

"Confusion" camouflage study

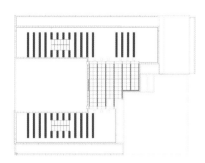

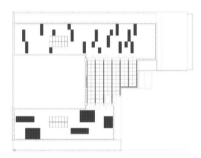

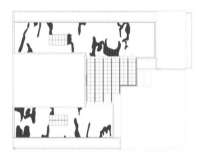

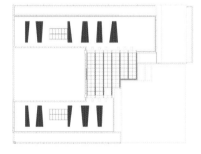

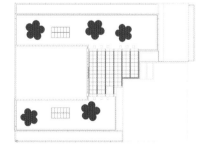

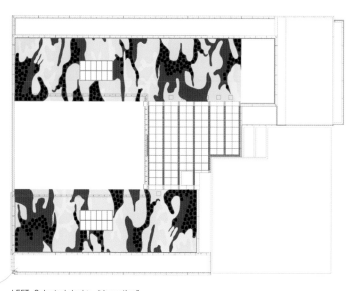

LEFT: Selected design: "deception"

RIGHT: Camouflage materials, initial palette

ack recycled rubber   White pebbles   Crushed glass   Foam header   Fiberglass grating   Shrub assembly   Black artificial rock   White artificial rock

Camouflage materials, final palette

something so strange and far out that it wouldn't be clear what the hell it was. This scheme had great big daisy shapes floating on the roof like mutant giant lily pads.

JA: **There seems to be a consistent use of faux plants, rocks, and paving textures that ignores the phenomenological potential and inherent mutability of landscape media—characteristics that could play into ideas of deception, confusion, and so on. How does investigation of materiality enter into these schemes?**

KS: The materials have shifted a little bit but basically all four of the schemes I presented involved artificial rocks, artificial shrubs, and three colors of ground material (white, black, and crushed glass). The palette remained consistent in the four schemes. Although the design was more about the form and content than materiality, the materials do have content, and to emphasize the simulation

aspects of the design I chose materials that were artificial and iconic.

JA: **The client sell was more successful the second time around—why?**

KS: I created graphics and a quarter-scale model of each scheme (later these were on display in a small exhibition at the Harvard Graduate School of Design) and presented them to the museum. I met with Terence Riley, Peter Reed, Glenn Lowry, and others and we agreed that we would take two of the schemes to the co-op board to present: the rectilinear one and the curvilinear one—imitation and deception.

I pushed for those two, although I also liked the confusion scheme. But I thought that the imitation and deception approaches were the most true to the idea of camouflage that we were developing. I was leaning toward the curvilinear scheme, although during our meeting with MoMA

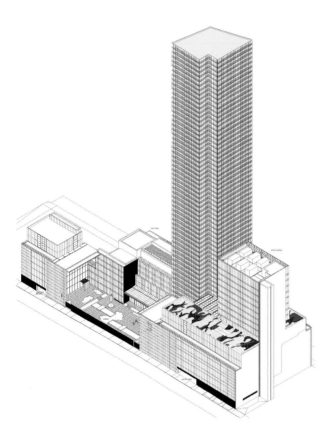

there were concerns about the curvilinear design being difficult to build. The rectilinear one would be simpler to construct, and everyone thought it might also be more palatable to the board members of the residential co-op because it's inherently more conservative. People understand minimalist geometry, and certainly it was more in keeping with the Taniguchi building. But that was exactly why I preferred the curvilinear scheme. I thought that it was more interestingly subversive about camouflage because it plays a reverse game of deception rather than simple imitation.

JA: **Many critics complain that the curvilinear is a default parti, a limiting, planimetric interpretation of a romantic, pastoral legacy. But really since the 1980s we've endured a regime of minimalist geometries and aggressive formalism that overlooks the figural power of site-specific, continuous topologies. How is the curvilinear scheme and its implication of a two-dimensional articulated ground plane more of a challenge to prevailing site aesthetics?**

KS: It has a whole series of levels that are interesting because so much of landscape architecture is uncritically involved in camouflaging. We're a profession of shrubbing things up, covering up mistakes, hiding and smoothing things, and contextualizing them. Usually, the camouflaging efforts within the profession are invisible. This scheme acknowledges the issue of camouflage and uses it critically as a visible element. But not everyone wants to hear about that.

I started the presentation to the co-op board by talking about the roof as a kind of Japanese garden. Part of the program stated that we couldn't have any live plants, we couldn't have any irrigation, we couldn't have any substantial weight, we couldn't have any physical attachments. There were also issues of a limited budget and little or no maintenance. Basically, things

Models of the four design study alternatives:
deception, decoy, imitation, confusion

opposite:
Deception

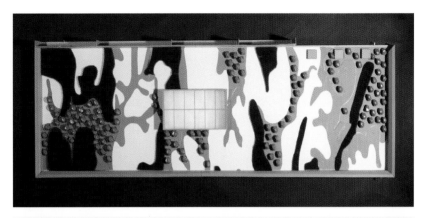

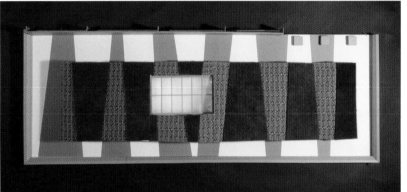

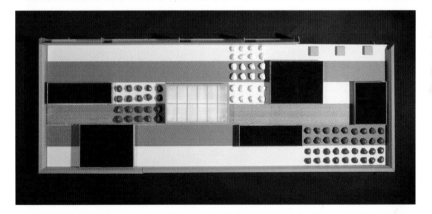

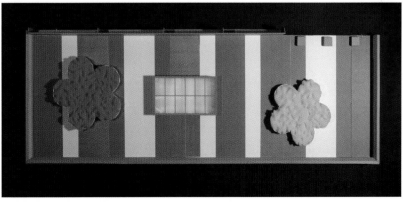

LEFT: Model of deception camouflage design

RIGHT: The camouflage patterns were initially traced from a
pair of hip-hop pants.

The roof garden in mid-construction, January 2005

had to be lightweight and set in place. It was inherently a dry garden, similar to the Japanese Zen garden, which is an abstraction of nature in some way. I continued by talking about the two schemes that we were going to present, a rectilinear geometry and a curvilinear geometry, showing them the gardens on top of Rockefeller Center as an example of a classical rectilinear geometry garden and Noguchi's work at UNESCO in Paris as an example of curvilinear, modern work. They loved it. The biggest hurdle was the synthetic palette of the garden.

I had built a small mock-up on the rooftop, which everyone could look down at. So instead of bringing an artificial shrub into the meeting, the materials were judged from a distance of forty or fifty feet, the actual viewing distance. From that perspective, you actually can't tell the difference between an artificial boxwood and a real one, and in fact, three years out, the artificial boxwoods are going to look better than a dead boxwood here

and there. Live plants would have difficulty surviving in the garden because of limited maintenance, limited soil, and the environmental conditions.

JA: **The scheme changed some between that meeting, where you presented the initial concept, and the final installation. How did value engineering effect specific construction details or change your interpretation of deception by design?**

KS: The shrub masses are made of fiberglass grating, and the bases are computer-numerically cut into pieces that fit together on the roof. I specified PVC pipes that go into PVC flanges which are bolted to the fiberglass grating to provide stems for the shrubs. These assemblies are heavy enough that they can just rest on the roof. Originally, I had planned to place the shrubs at a distance of twenty-four inches from each other, but this was eventually adjusted to thirty or thirty-six inches

Detail showing artificial rocks

Opposite: Aerial view of north and south roofs

to save money—ironically the artificial boxwood plants were more expensive than live plants. This adjustment saved $40,000, but a study also showed that the new spacing actually worked better. In a real landscape with real plants you would want the shrubs to be placed close to each other, so that they can grow together as a mass, but here, having the shrubs read as individual elements worked because it made the design more synthetic.

The artificial rocks I used are a brand that people in the suburbs use to hide their utilities. Basically they're camouflaging elements in the landscape. Across the rooftop I laid a series of runners to which the rocks were bolted. Placed over the runners is a thin layer of ground cover. The black ground cover was originally Mexican black pebbles because that was what Taniguchi's office had specified, but to save money I decided to use ground tires—recycled rubber, a material recommended by the landscape contractor. The white surface, made of crushed white stone, is the only

natural material, although it could be called into question whether this material is actually natural or not at this point. The blue surface is crushed glass, which could also be considered a natural material. It also calls into question what's authentic and what's simulated.

Some of the changes I made to the original scheme happened to cut costs. For example, the headers were going to be brick in order to relate to the historic context by choosing the same material Philip Johnson used, but instead I ended up using CNC-milled structural Styrofoam. In historic preservation work a lot of detailing, such as cornices, is made out of this material, usually with a finish that looks like limestone or another stone. Here it is treated with a spray-on hardening surface that's really strong and painted the color of brick. All the shapes in the curvilinear plan are translated arcs, tangents, and straight lines taken from a camouflage pattern that was traced from a pair of hip-hop, skate-boarder pants. I wanted to make the

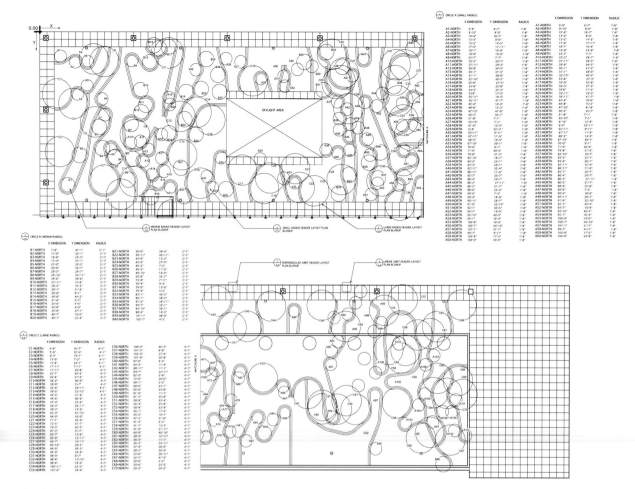

Roof garden layout, construction documents

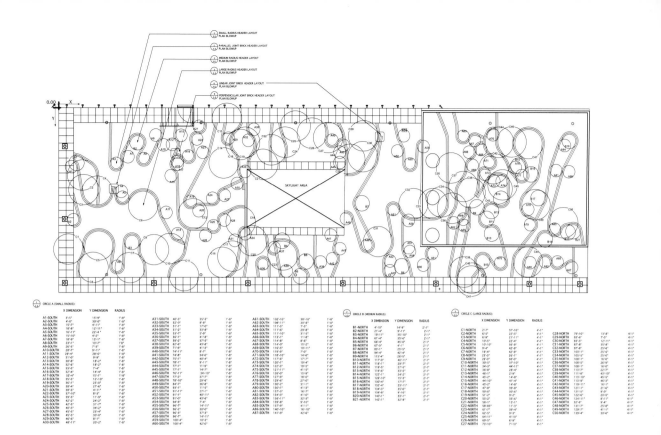

SMALL RADIUS HEADER LAYOUT
PLAN BLOWUP

PARALLEL JOINT BRICK HEADER LAYOUT
PLAN BLOWUP

MEDIUM RADIUS HEADER LAYOUT
PLAN BLOWUP

LARGE RADIUS HEADER LAYOUT
PLAN BLOWUP

LINEAR JOINT BRICK HEADER LAYOUT

PERPENDICULAR JOINT BRICK HEADER LAYOUT
PLAN BLOWUP

SKYLIGHT AREA

CIRCLE A (SMALL RADIUS):

	X DIMENSION	Y DIMENSION	RADIUS		X DIMENSION	Y DIMENSION	RADIUS		X DIMENSION	Y DIMENSION	RADIUS
A1-SOUTH	3'-5"	15'-8"	1'-8"	A31-SOUTH	40'-3"	35'-5"	1'-8"	A61-SOUTH	102'-10"	38'-10"	1'-8"
A2-SOUTH	4'-0"	30'-0"	1'-8"	A32-SOUTH	52'-0"	8'-8"	1'-8"	A62-SOUTH	108'-11"	30'-8"	1'-8"
A3-SOUTH	15'-7"	5'-0"	1'-8"	A33-SOUTH	51'-1"	17'-0"	1'-8"	A63-SOUTH	111'-6"	7'-5"	1'-8"
A4-SOUTH	18'-8"	12'-11"	1'-8"	A34-SOUTH	51'-2"	33'-8"	1'-8"	A64-SOUTH	111'-6"	29'-8"	1'-8"
A5-SOUTH	16'-11"	22'-4"	1'-8"	A35-SOUTH	53'-7"	5'-9"	1'-8"	A65-SOUTH	111'-10"	31'-5"	1'-8"
A6-SOUTH	15'-10"	4'-2"	1'-8"	A36-SOUTH	56'-1"	41'-8"	1'-8"	A66-SOUTH	113'-1"	11'-8"	1'-8"
A7-SOUTH	18'-9"	13'-1"	1'-8"	A37-SOUTH	59'-2"	37'-5"	1'-8"	A67-SOUTH	114'-8"	8'-6"	1'-8"
A8-SOUTH	23'-1"	13'-7"	1'-8"	A38-SOUTH	62'-4"	49'-8"	1'-8"	A68-SOUTH	114'-0"	15'-2"	1'-8"
A9-SOUTH	26'-5"	7'-5"	1'-8"	A39-SOUTH	71'-4"	41'-3"	1'-8"	A69-SOUTH	116'-5"	10'-11"	1'-8"
A10-SOUTH	28'-7"	9'-11"	1'-8"	A40-SOUTH	74'-11"	8'-7"	1'-8"	A70-SOUTH	119'-6"	7'-6"	1'-8"
A11-SOUTH	29'-4"	28'-0"	1'-8"	A41-SOUTH	74'-8"	34'-0"	1'-8"	A71-SOUTH	118'-10"	14'-6"	1'-8"
A12-SOUTH	31'-0"	9'-9"	1'-8"	A42-SOUTH	75'-1"	40'-4"	1'-8"	A72-SOUTH	117'-6"	17'-7"	1'-8"
A13-SOUTH	30'-8"	18'-2"	1'-8"	A43-SOUTH	78'-1"	9'-11"	1'-8"	A73-SOUTH	120'-1"	19'-4"	1'-8"
A14-SOUTH	32'-4"	18'-2"	1'-8"	A44-SOUTH	77'-1"	11'-8"	1'-8"	A74-SOUTH	122'-0"	19'-5"	1'-8"
A15-SOUTH	33'-5"	7'-4"	1'-8"	A45-SOUTH	77'-1"	14'-7"	1'-8"	A75-SOUTH	121'-11"	41'-5"	1'-8"
A16-SOUTH	31'-2"	14'-4"	1'-8"	A46-SOUTH	76'-11"	34'-10"	1'-8"	A76-SOUTH	126'-0"	15'-9"	1'-8"
A17-SOUTH	32'-4"	15'-1"	1'-8"	A47-SOUTH	77'-2"	37'-7"	1'-8"	A77-SOUTH	127'-6"	18'-0"	1'-8"
A18-SOUTH	35'-5"	12'-10"	1'-8"	A48-SOUTH	78'-10"	29'-6"	1'-8"	A78-SOUTH	129'-6"	27'-0"	1'-8"
A19-SOUTH	36'-1"	25'-0"	1'-8"	A49-SOUTH	84'-7"	36'-8"	1'-8"	A79-SOUTH	130'-2"	31'-1"	1'-8"
A20-SOUTH	38'-4"	27'-4"	1'-8"	A50-SOUTH	93'-1"	11'-5"	1'-8"	A80-SOUTH	130'-1"	41'-3"	1'-8"
A21-SOUTH	38'-5"	4'-11"	1'-8"	A51-SOUTH	91'-11"	27'-1"	1'-8"	A81-SOUTH	137'-9"	14'-7"	1'-8"
A22-SOUTH	37'-10"	8'-5"	1'-8"	A52-SOUTH	91'-1"	40'-11"	1'-8"	A82-SOUTH	134'-3"	41'-0"	1'-8"
A23-SOUTH	39'-5"	11'-9"	1'-8"	A53-SOUTH	91'-0"	43'-6"	1'-8"	A83-SOUTH	136'-11"	32'-3"	1'-8"
A24-SOUTH	42'-2"	24'-2"	1'-8"	A54-SOUTH	94'-6"	7'-4"	1'-8"	A84-SOUTH	139'-8"	9'-10"	1'-8"
A25-SOUTH	42'-5"	31'-7"	1'-8"	A55-SOUTH	96'-7"	14'-11"	1'-8"	A85-SOUTH	137'-9"	41'-1"	1'-8"
A26-SOUTH	40'-3"	34'-2"	1'-8"	A56-SOUTH	96'-2"	30'-0"	1'-8"	A86-SOUTH	140'-10"	16'-10"	1'-8"
A27-SOUTH	45'-5"	23'-4"	1'-8"	A57-SOUTH	96'-3"	37'-3"	1'-8"	A87-SOUTH	141'-9"	42'-6"	1'-8"
A28-SOUTH	45'-5"	30'-0"	1'-8"	A58-SOUTH	96'-7"	14'-11"	1'-8"				
A29-SOUTH	46'-6"	8'-1"	1'-8"	A59-SOUTH	100'-4"	10'-3"	1'-8"				
A30-SOUTH	46'-11"	20'-2"	1'-8"	A60-SOUTH	100'-4"	42'-0"	1'-8"				

CIRCLE B (MEDIUM RADIUS):

	X DIMENSION	Y DIMENSION	RADIUS
B1-NORTH	4'-10"	14'-9"	2'-1"
B2-NORTH	21'-4"	9'-11"	2'-1"
B3-NORTH	19'-11"	55'-10"	2'-1"
B4-NORTH	61'-4"	35'-4"	2'-1"
B5-NORTH	66'-4"	45'-0"	2'-1"
B6-NORTH	67'-5"	4'-1"	2'-1"
B7-NORTH	83'-1"	25'-5"	2'-1"
B8-NORTH	84'-4"	42'-4"	2'-1"
B9-NORTH	115'-4"	26'-5"	2'-1"
B10-NORTH	117'-0"	40'-11"	2'-1"
B11-NORTH	118'-1"	29'-7"	2'-1"
B12-NORTH	119'-0"	27'-3"	2'-1"
B13-NORTH	119'-6"	33'-5"	2'-1"
B14-NORTH	122'-1"	24'-2"	2'-1"
B15-NORTH	126'-10"	15'-9"	2'-1"
B16-NORTH	130'-4"	17'-7"	2'-1"
B17-NORTH	132'-4"	23'-11"	2'-1"
B18-NORTH	134'-3"	35'-0"	2'-1"
B19-NORTH	139'-6"	9'-10"	2'-1"
B20-NORTH	140'-1"	33'-1"	2'-1"
B21-NORTH	142'-1"	32'-0"	2'-1"

CIRCLE C (LARGE RADIUS):

	X DIMENSION	Y DIMENSION	RADIUS		X DIMENSION	Y DIMENSION	RADIUS
C1-NORTH	2'-7"	57'-10"	4'-1"	C28-NORTH	79'-10"	15'-8"	4'-1"
C2-NORTH	6'-5"	22'-5"	4'-1"	C29-NORTH	83'-6"	7'-5"	4'-1"
C3-NORTH	6'-9"	21'-11"	4'-1"	C30-NORTH	83'-5"	12'-11"	4'-1"
C4-NORTH	10'-5"	22'-4"	4'-1"	C31-NORTH	101'-10"	35'-8"	4'-1"
C5-NORTH	10'-10"	36'-8"	4'-1"	C32-NORTH	97'-4"	25'-4"	4'-1"
C6-NORTH	9'-4"	42'-9"	4'-1"	C33-NORTH	103'-1"	25'-6"	4'-1"
C7-NORTH	23'-0"	26'-1"	4'-1"	C34-NORTH	105'-5"	25'-0"	4'-1"
C8-NORTH	23'-0"	38'-0"	4'-1"	C35-NORTH	108'-5"	18'-0"	4'-1"
C9-NORTH	30'-5"	37'-10"	4'-1"	C36-NORTH	108'-5"	26'-0"	4'-1"
C10-NORTH	34'-0"	44'-11"	4'-1"	C37-NORTH	108'-1"	11'-0"	4'-1"
C11-NORTH	36'-4"	28'-4"	4'-1"	C38-NORTH	113'-7"	22'-7"	4'-1"
C12-NORTH	46'-1"	2'-0"	4'-1"	C39-NORTH	111'-6"	43'-10"	4'-1"
C13-NORTH	46'-1"	2'-0"	4'-1"	C40-NORTH	113'-10"	45'-6"	4'-1"
C14-NORTH	45'-2"	14'-8"	4'-1"	C41-NORTH	113'-8"	35'-8"	4'-1"
C15-NORTH	44'-10"	41'-4"	4'-1"	C42-NORTH	119'-11"	14'-1"	4'-1"
C16-NORTH	45'-2"	14'-8"	4'-1"	C43-NORTH	121'-1"	21'-6"	4'-1"
C17-NORTH	47'-8"	35'-8"	4'-1"	C44-NORTH	121'-5"	9'-0"	4'-1"
C18-NORTH	50'-0"	30'-4"	4'-1"	C45-NORTH	122'-6"	20'-5"	4'-1"
C19-NORTH	51'-2"	9'-2"	4'-1"	C46-NORTH	124'-11"	8'-11"	4'-1"
C20-NORTH	53'-2"	35'-4"	4'-1"	C47-NORTH	32'-6"	9'-4"	4'-1"
C21-NORTH	56'-1"	15'-1"	4'-1"	C48-NORTH	131'-7"	25'-8"	4'-1"
C22-NORTH	58'-83"	11'-3"	4'-1"	C49-NORTH	129'-1"	9'-4"	4'-1"
C23-NORTH	61'-7"	35'-4"	4'-1"	C50-NORTH	139'-4"	30'-6"	4'-1"
C24-NORTH	62'-5"	9'-5"	4'-1"				
C25-NORTH	64'-11"	41'-10"	4'-1"				
C26-NORTH	69'-5"	6'-9"	4'-1"				
C27-NORTH	73'-10"	7'-1"	4'-1"				

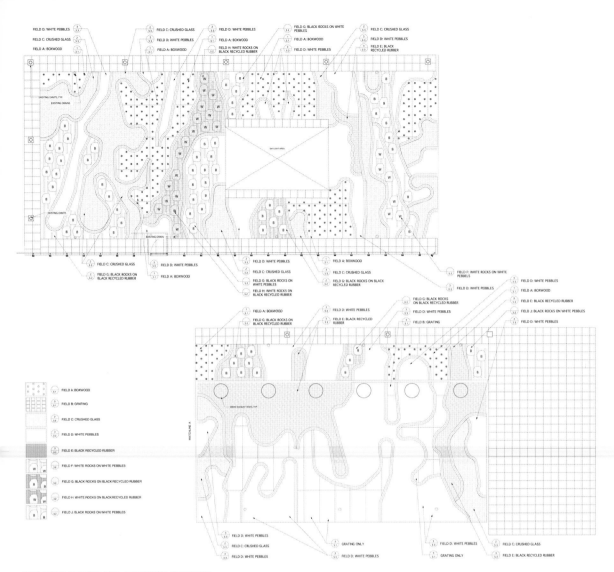

Roof garden materials plan, construction documents

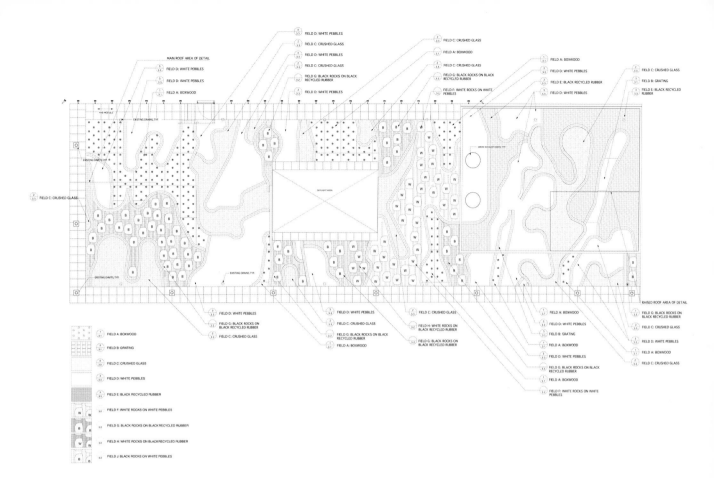

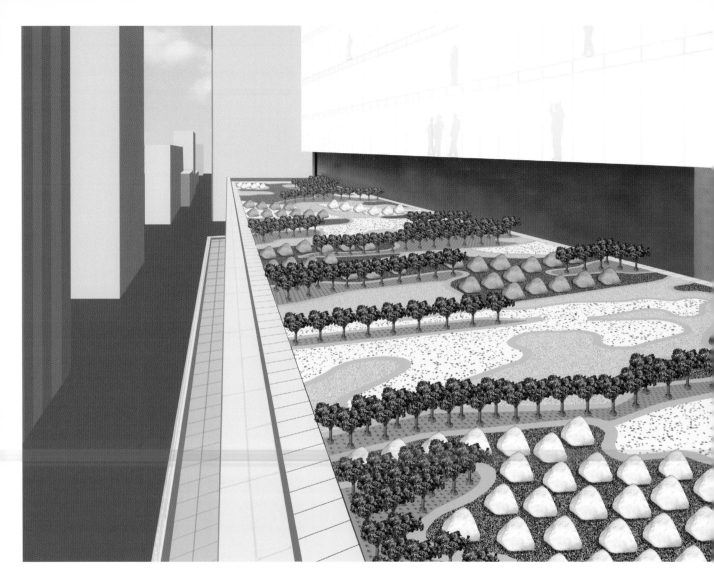

Montage of final design

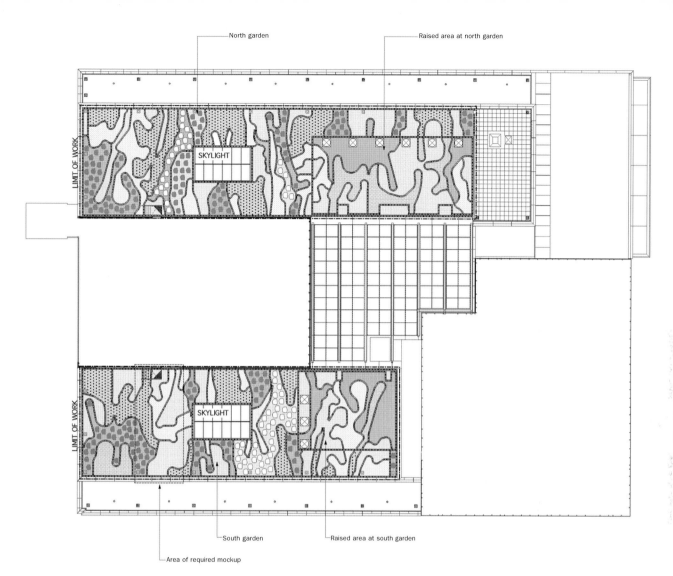

North garden

Raised area at north garden

LIMIT OF WORK

SKYLIGHT

LIMIT OF WORK

SKYLIGHT

South garden

Raised area at south garden

Area of required mockup

Composite plan showing north and south roofs

South roof, view from 40 West 53rd Street

Mock-up of roof garden layout, January 2004

camouflage a little more synthetic so I reduced the pattern to a kind of roadway engineering. There are three different curve radii and three different line-segment and intersection conditions. To transfer the pattern onto the roof, it was divided into a series of simple units, which were factory-cut from standard sheet sizes into a palette of parts, numbered at the factory, put together on site, and glued down.

As I was concerned about the integrity of the curvilinear forms, my office staff and I mocked up about a fifth of the area on one side of the roof with chalk and string lines. In half a day we laid out the geometry of one substantial area of the design so we could see how the forms fit and get a sense of the scale. We looked down at it from the tower, which was kind of reassuring. We also discovered we had some dimensioning issues in the rooftop layout, which needed to be corrected. These little adjustments, and in some ways also the things we had to do to bring the budget

down, made the project conceptually stronger. The whole process of being forced to go back to the client with a completely new idea after the first design was rejected and work through the issues of the rejected proposal resulted in a better design concept. And while I'm not a big fan of value engineering, in this case it clarified the material palette and made the project stronger conceptually and materially.

JA: **In retrospect, what got sacrificed when you let go of the first proposal, the spinning daisies?**

KS: The MoMA team loved the first scheme. Terry Riley liked it because it used an iconic element taken out of context. Peter Reed liked it because it hovered between pop art and minimalism. When Peter talks about landscape architecture, his approach is to speak about landscape design relative to the tug between surrealism and cubism. I don't know if those quite translate to pop art and

minimalism but Peter thought it was interesting
that on one level the scheme was pop because
you've got the iconic daisy, the found object.
And on another level, the design was purely minimalist as the big blocks of color made up a minimal color field that underlies the operative level of
the spinning and turning objects in the wind. But
in the end, I think the deception/camouflage garden hovers in the same way, in this case between a
kind of utilitarian industrial-design appropriation
strategy and Japanese garden abstraction.

East River Ferry Landings

New York, New York

In 2001 the city of New York selected five design firms to submit proposals for the East River waterfront alongside the six ferry landings including Thirty-fourth Street in Midtown. The area of intervention was a ninety-foot-long strip of seawall and a twenty-foot-wide right of way owned by the city. The program was to create a pedestrian environment that would extend existing riverside circulation through the site. In relation to a bridged walkway designed by architects Sheila Kennedy and Frano Violich, Ken Smith developed an urban ecological system that revives atavistic plantings—grasses that once prospered along the sloped banks of the river—within a constructed nature of folded, unmistakably contemporary planters.

JA: **Describe how you got involved with this project.**

KS: The city picked five firms that were invited to submit proposals. Besides me, the architectural firm Kennedy & Violich and three other architectural practices were on the list. I was the only landscape architect. I knew Frano Violich and Sheila Kennedy from teaching at the Harvard Graduate School of Design, and one day Frano called me up to ask whether I was interested in joining forces. I really respected their work. So we became a collaborative team and basically picked off the competition that way. Kennedy & Violich's designs for buildings and structures are based on a kind of systems approach: they think about occupying surfaces in terms of movement. In their scheme for the project there is a system of furnishings—all utilizable in some way—that move through the site and a system of canopies, which provide protection. In response, I started to think about the landscape as a system, as an ecological system consisting of individual planters that might reclaim the riparian edge of the river.

Kennedy and Violich were great to work with. They never once said, "No, you should be doing it this way." We basically developed our own ideas in a common vocabulary and program. The

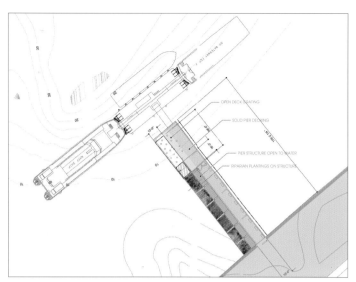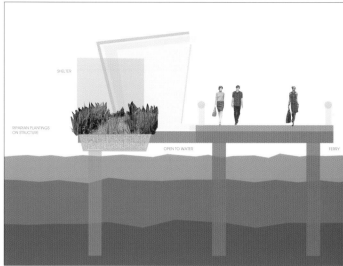

Initial concept studies for the East River Ferry Landings were based on a set of planters that carried into the water.

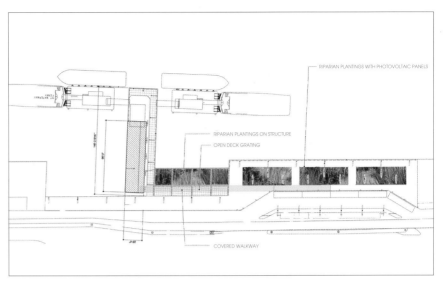

RIPARIAN PLANTINGS WITH PHOTOVOLTAIC PANELS

RIPARIAN PLANTINGS ON STRUCTURE

OPEN DECK GRATING

COVERED WALKWAY

Initial concept study

substructure was designed by engineers, so we both responded to a structural armature, with Kennedy & Violich's buildings oftentimes sitting on piers. They were working with a series of organic forms on their roof structures. These are folded surfaces, and while my own folded forms are much more angular than theirs, the combined design results in a dialogue of folded or warped forms.

JA: **This high-profile project has some real limitations in terms of what you, as the landscape architect, can achieve. Describe the site issues you are dealing with.**

KS: The project underwent severe value engineering in which a lot of my design was cut. We also had some difficulty getting environmental approval. I find it ironic that the riparian marsh planters, which do the most environmental good, are so difficult to get approved. It is the part of my project that most speaks to the loss of the natural riparian edge

and environmental issues. But while we can get permits to build platforms for people to walk on and for boats to tie up to, the riparian plantings, which actually do some good in terms of visibility and communicate the importance and loss of the riparian environment, are the pieces that are getting most critiqued. It's very frustrating. We still don't have all the approvals necessary to construct the marsh planters, and this part of the project is in danger of being deleted. It just breaks my heart.

I started work on this project in 2001 with some very simple Photoshop studies. At the beginning there was a set of forms that carried into the water. As the project moved forward, my staff did a lot of research on soils, drainage, and other aspects of river ecosystems. The structure evolved from an original design of sloped planters made of wood piles (expecting we would have pier construction with wood piles), to one of steel H-piles once the engineer decided that steel made the most sense structurally and economically.

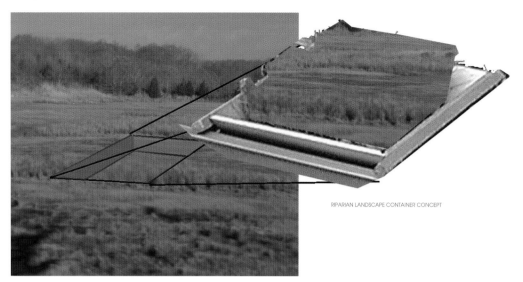

RIPARIAN LANDSCAPE CONTAINER CONCEPT

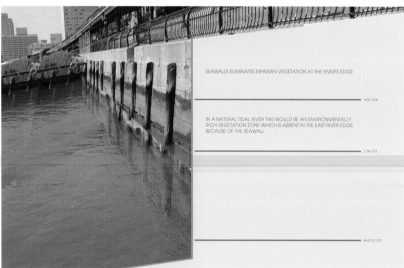

SEAWALLS ELIMINATES RIPARIAN VEGETATION AT THE RIVER'S EDGE

HIGH-TIDE

IN A NATURAL TIDAL RIVER THIS WOULD BE AN ENVIRONMENTALLY
RICH VEGETATION ZONE WHICH IS ABSENT IN THE EAST RIVER EDGE
BECAUSE OF THE SEAWALL

LOW-TIDE

MUD-FLOOR

Before the design was presented to the client, KSLA
collected information on soils, drainage, and other aspects
of river ecosystems that pertained to the East River site.

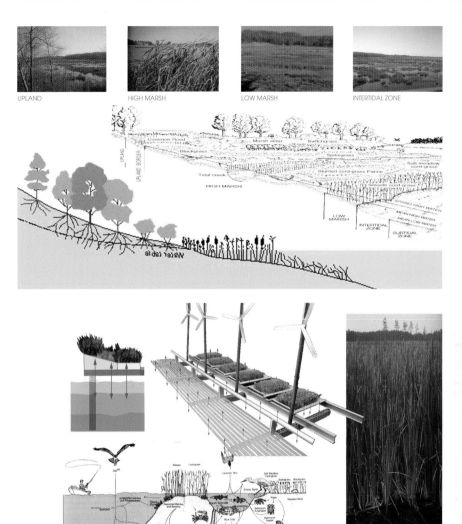

UPLAND HIGH MARSH LOW MARSH INTERTIDAL ZONE

Initial concept studies

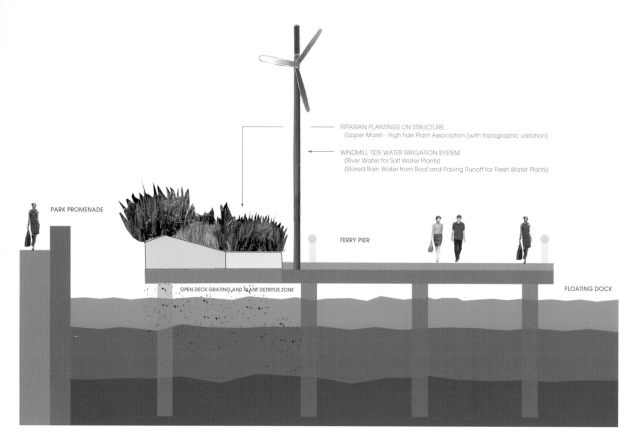

RIPARIAN PLANTINGS ON STRUCTURE
(Upper Marsh - High tide Plant Association (with topographic variation)

WINDMILL TIDE WATER IRRIGATION SYSTEM
(River Water for Salt Water Plants)
(Stored Rain Water from Roof and Paving Runoff for Fresh Water Plants)

PARK PROMENADE

FERRY PIER

FLOATING DOCK

OPEN DECK GRATING AND PLANT DETRITUS ZONE

The planted boxes have elevated and low areas mimicking a
natural river slope. An artificial irrigation system pumps river
water into the boxes.

opposite:
Montage of initial design study

JA: **The warped rectangular form has something in common with the pleating of the Hiriya landfill project, although the scales are vastly different.**

KS: Yes, this similarity reflects my move toward vertical green and folding forms. Creating a topography was important to me because the project was about repairing an edge, and the riparian edge is inherently a graded slope. In the East River, the tidal fluctuation is about six feet between high and low tide. In a natural condition the river's gradated slope dissipates the energy of the river's movement allowing tidal plant communities of primarily spartina grass to thrive. The ecology of the East River has been altered through land filling and construction of sea walls, and today's currents would not allow these types of communities to exist without some kind of protective structure. Simply planting spartina grass in a slope on the river wouldn't work in this altered environment because the river

currents would just scour them away. The planters are actually necessary to protect the grass. In the given space there wasn't enough room to create a true gradated slope that would support the range of low marsh, high marsh, and upland border. Instead, as a sculptural notion, I developed a folding structure that has elevated areas and lower ones. An irrigation system pumps river water into the planted boxes, a kind of artificial tide, which results in a differentiation of plant selection sorting itself out within the planters. Necessarily, the lower areas, where more moisture gathers, have a greater population of mussels and things like that. At high tide these areas will get flooded.

JA: **The planting boxes make what used to be a natural condition—vegetated shoreline—possible again, but in a manner that reflects the engineered condition. Is there some inherent wrong-doing in this? The freshwater irrigation needed for the spartina grasses and foreign,**

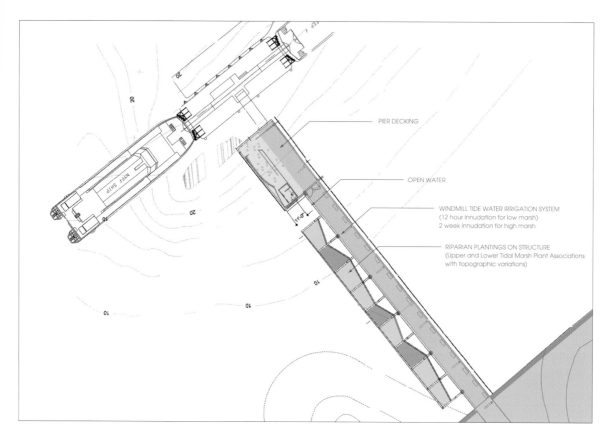

PIER DECKING

OPEN WATER

WINDMILL TIDE WATER IRRIGATION SYSTEM
(12 hour innudation for low marsh)
2 week innudation for high marsh

RIPARIAN PLANTINGS ON STRUCTURE
(Upper and Lower Tidal Marsh Plant Associations
with topographic variations)

As the marsh planters were developed in response to the river conditions, instead of being submerged, where strong currents would damage the plantings, they were raised slightly above high tide.

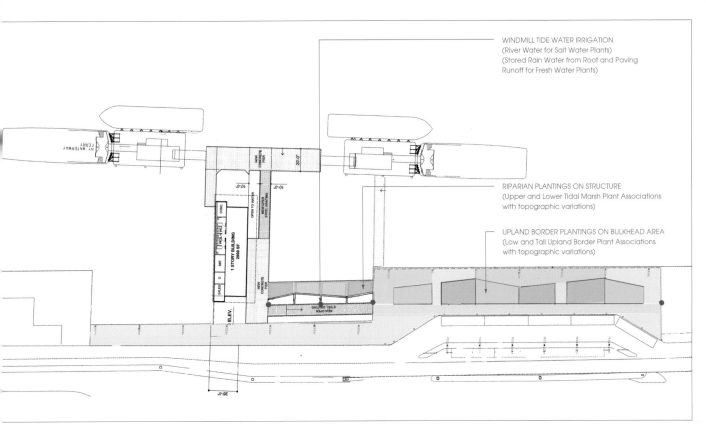

WINDMILL TIDE WATER IRRIGATION
(River Water for Salt Water Plants)
(Stored Rain Water from Roof and Paving
Runoff for Fresh Water Plants)

RIPARIAN PLANTINGS ON STRUCTURE
(Upper and Lower Tidal Marsh Plant Associations
with topographic variations)

UPLAND BORDER PLANTINGS ON BULKHEAD AREA
(Low and Tall Upland Border Plant Associations
with topographic variations)

Study for marsh planters at 34th Street

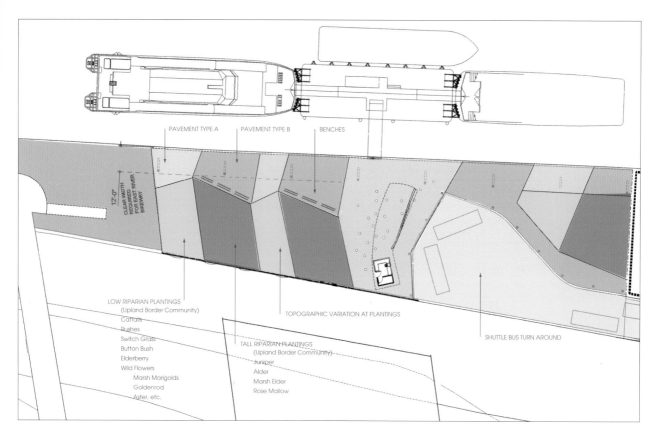

PAVEMENT TYPE A   PAVEMENT TYPE B   BENCHES

12'-0"
CLEAR WIDTH
REQUIRED FOR EAST RIVER
BIKEWAY

LOW RIPARIAN PLANTINGS
(Upland Border Community)
Cattails
Rushes
Switch Grass
Button Bush
Elderberry
Wild Flowers
    Marsh Marigolds
    Goldenrod
    Aster, etc.

TOPOGRAPHIC VARIATION AT PLANTINGS

TALL RIPARIAN PLANTINGS
(Upland Border Community)
Juniper
Alder
Marsh Elder
Rose Mallow

SHUTTLE BUS TURN AROUND

Study for marsh planters at 65th Street

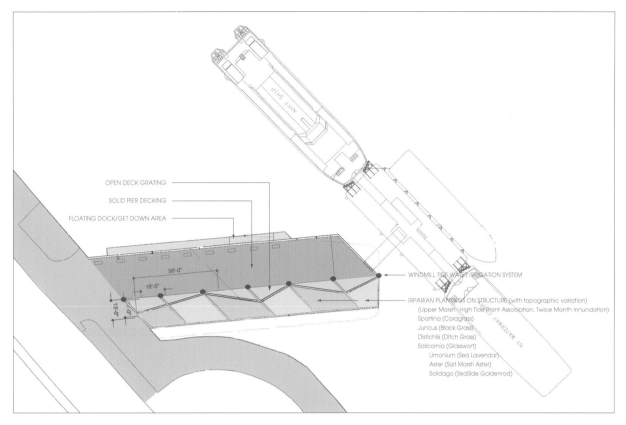

OPEN DECK GRATING

SOLID PIER DECKING

FLOATING DOCK/GET DOWN AREA

58'-0"

16'-0"

13'-0"

NYFF SHIP

NY WATERWAY TERMINAL

WINDMILL TIDE WATER IRRIGATION SYSTEM

RIPARIAN PLANTINGS ON STRUCTURE (with topographic variation)
(Upper Marsh - High Tide Plant Association, Twice Month Innundation)
Spartina (Cordgrass)
Juncus (Black Grass)
Distichlis (Ditch Grass)
Salicornia (Glasswort)
Limonium (Sea Lavendar)
Aster (Salt Marsh Aster)
Solidago (SeaSide Goldenrod)

TOP: Second-pass design study for marsh
planters at 90th Street
BOTTOM: Model of initial design study

overleaf:
Montage of second-pass design study

fortified planting soils will enter into the river system, and one could imagine, if this project served as a model for miles of shoreline, the river water's nutrient balance would be disturbed.

KS: Well, this project is intended for a stretch of river that is already irreparably out of balance. It addresses the issue of how we respond to an altered riparian environment and how we can create an awareness of the problem. Because of the river's bulkhead walls and altered currents, it is impossible to grow a riparian marsh in natural conditions here, so I resorted to designing a planter system that would allow bringing back the Spartina community under controlled and protected conditions. The planter box is a very practical solution, but to make it work in the altered ecology of the East River it is necessary to introduce irrigation using both brackish water and a back-up system of fresh water to support the plantings. The planter boxes are designed to receive only limited tidal flushing, in order to protect the plantings from the damage of strong currents. Supplemental water is pumped from the river and distributed through a system of open troughs and spouts to provide an artificial tidal influx of brackish water and nutrients. There is also an auxiliary back-up system of fresh water in case there is a problem with the brackish water system. I designed the latter to be a visible component of the planters. It's part of our attempt to expose the structure of what we created, to reveal the systems that propagate and sustain the plants. I wanted to show the mechanics and the complexity of the materials and systems, so they become an accessible part of understanding the landscape. I'm not interested in covering up and denying these things.

JA: **Do you identify this concern with revealing structure and function as a modernist strain in your work?**

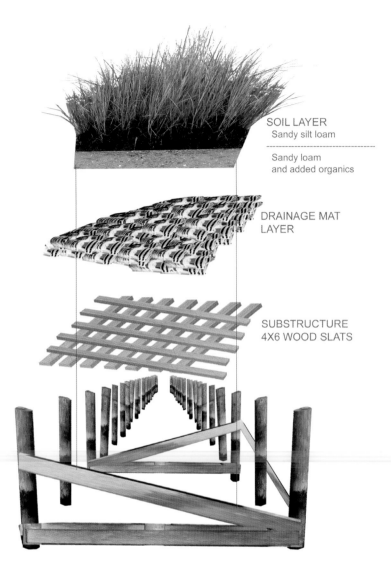

SOIL LAYER
Sandy silt loam

Sandy loam
and added organics

DRAINAGE MAT
LAYER

SUBSTRUCTURE
4X6 WOOD SLATS

Construction concept of second-pass design study

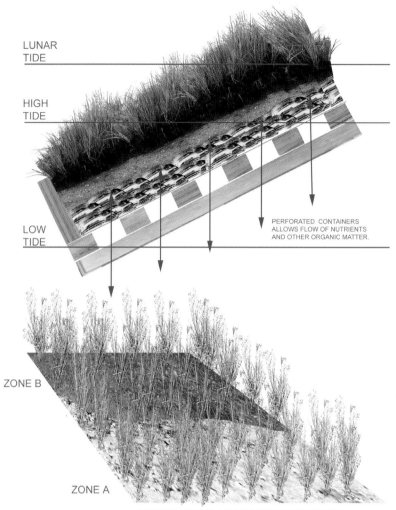

LUNAR
TIDE

HIGH
TIDE

LOW
TIDE

PERFORATED CONTAINERS
ALLOWS FLOW OF NUTRIENTS
AND OTHER ORGANIC MATTER.

ZONE B

ZONE A

VEGETATION PLAN LAYOUT USING PLUGS
OR PRE-VEGETATED MATS

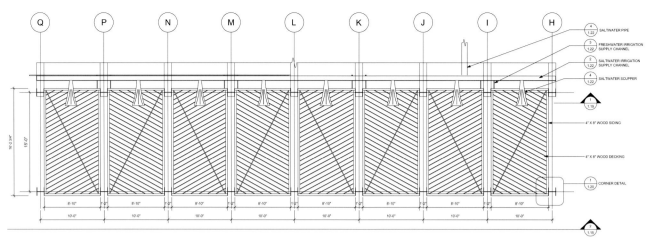

Q P N M L K J I H

4 1.22 SALTWATER PIPE
3 1.22 FRESHWATER IRRIGATION SUPPLY CHANNEL
2 1.22 SALTWATER IRRIGATION SUPPLY CHANNEL
4 1.22 SALTWATER SCUPPER

4" X 8" WOOD SIDING

4" X 8" WOOD DECKING

1 1.20 CORNER DETAIL

8'-10" 1'-2" 8'-10" 1'-2" 8'-10" 1'-2" 8'-10" 1'-2" 8'-10" 1'-2" 8'-10" 1'-2" 8'-10"
10'-0" 10'-0" 10'-0" 10'-0" 10'-0" 10'-0" 10'-0" 10'-0"

16'-2 3/4"
15'-0"

1 MARSHPLANTER
PLAN   1/4" = 1' - 0"

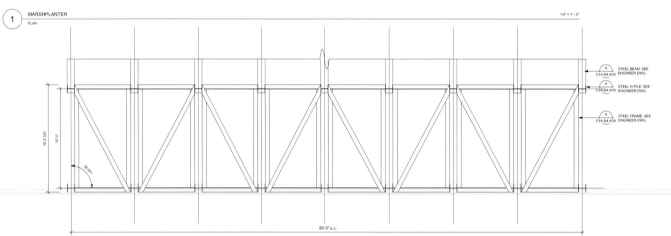

A E34:SM-409 STEEL BEAM: SEE ENGINEER DWG
A E34:SM-409 STEEL H-PILE: SEE ENGINEER DWG
A E34:SM-409 STEEL FRAME: SEE ENGINEER DWG

16'-2 3/4"
15'-0"

80'-0" o.c.

2 MARSHPLANTER SUBSTRUCTURE
PLAN   1/4" = 1' - 0"

Construction documents

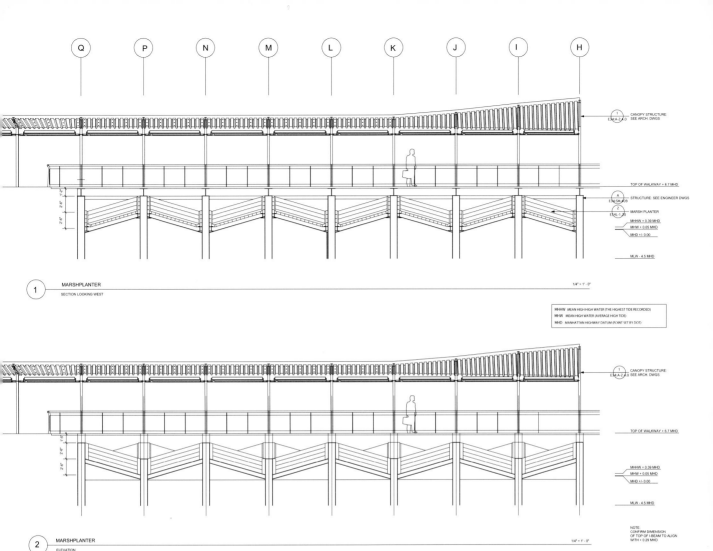

Q P N M L K J I H

CANOPY STRUCTURE
SEE ARCH. DWGS

1
E34-A-2.0

TOP OF WALKWAY + 6.7 MHD

STRUCTURE: SEE ENGINEER DWGS

A
E34-SM-509

MARSH PLANTER

2
E34L-1.20

MHHW + 0.39 MHD
MHW + 0.05 MHD
MHD +/- 0.00

MLW - 4.5 MHD

1'-2" 2'-6" 2'-6"

1 MARSHPLANTER
SECTION LOOKING WEST

1/4" = 1' - 0"

MHHW   MEAN HIGH HIGH WATER (THE HIGHEST TIDE RECORDED)
MHW   MEAN HIGH WATER (AVERAGE HIGH TIDE)
MHD   MANHATTAN HIGHWAY DATUM (POINT SET BY DOT)

CANOPY STRUCTURE
SEE ARCH. DWGS

1
E34-A-2.0

TOP OF WALKWAY + 6.7 MHD

MHHW + 0.39 MHD
MHW + 0.05 MHD
MHD +/- 0.00

MLW - 4.5 MHD

1'-2" 2'-6" 2'-6"

NOTE:
CONFIRM DIMENSION
OF TOP OF I-BEAM TO ALIGN
WITH + 0.29 MHD

2 MARSHPLANTER
ELEVATION

1/4" = 1' - 0"

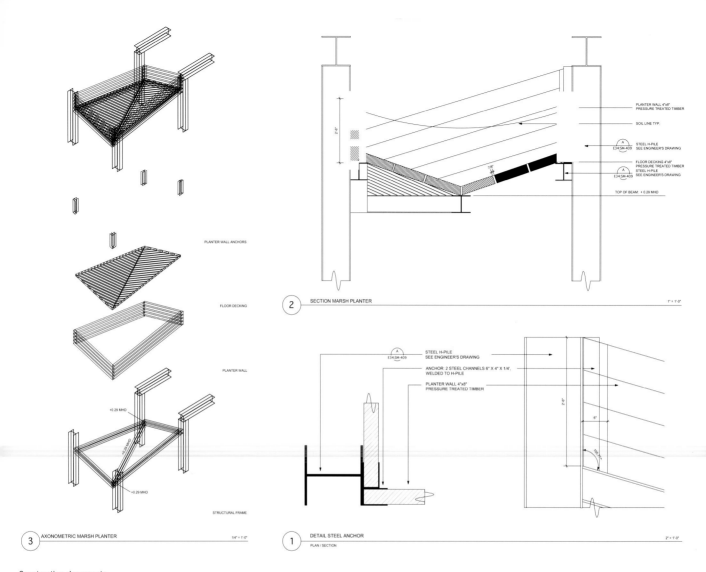

PLANTER WALL ANCHORS

FLOOR DECKING

PLANTER WALL

+0.29 MHD

+0.29 MHD

+0.29 MHD

STRUCTURAL FRAME

3 AXONOMETRIC MARSH PLANTER   1/4" = 1'-0"

PLANTER WALL 4"x8"
PRESSURE TREATED TIMBER

SOIL LINE TYP.

STEEL H-PILE
SEE ENGINEER'S DRAWING
E34-SM-409

FLOOR DECKING 4"x8"
PRESSURE TREATED TIMBER
STEEL H-PILE
SEE ENGINEER'S DRAWING
E34-SM-409

TOP OF BEAM: + 0.29 MHD

2 SECTION MARSH PLANTER   1" = 1'-0"

STEEL H-PILE
SEE ENGINEER'S DRAWING
E34-SM-409

ANCHOR: 2 STEEL CHANNELS 6" X 4" X 1/4",
WELDED TO H-PILE

PLANTER WALL 4"x8"
PRESSURE TREATED TIMBER

1 DETAIL STEEL ANCHOR   2" = 1'-0"
   PLAN / SECTION

Construction documents

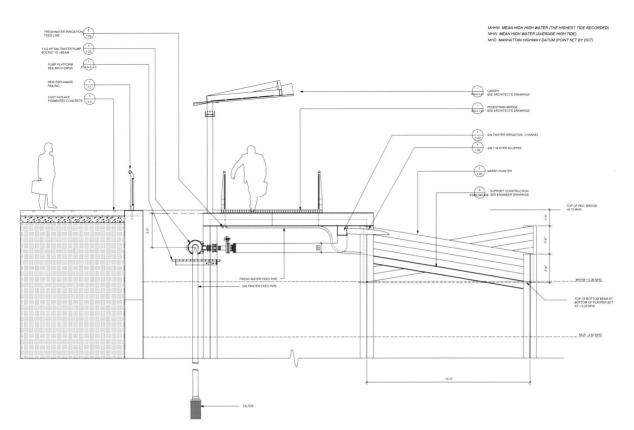

FRESHWATER IRRIGATION
FEED LINE

1 1/2 HP SALTWATER PUMP
BOLTED TO I-BEAM

PUMP PLATFORM
SEE ARCH DWGS

NEW ESPLANADE
RAILING

CAST IN PLACE
PIGMENTED CONCRETE

CANOPY
SEE ARCHITECT'S DRAWINGS

PEDESTRIAN BRIDGE
SEE ARCHITECT'S DRAWINGS

SALTWATER IRRIGATION CHANNEL

SALT WATER SCUPPER

MARSH PLANTER

SUPPORT CONSTRUCTION
SEE ENGINEER DRAWINGS

TOP OF PED. BRIDGE
+6.70 MHD

FRESH WATER FEED PIPE

SALTWATER FEED PIPE

MHHW + 0.29 MHD

TOP OF BOTTOM BEAM AT
BOTTOM OF PLANTER SET
AT +0.29 MHD

MLW -4.50 MHD

FILTER

KS: Yes. Basically you have the form of the function. But I'm also interested in the overlap between structure and the symbolic. If you look at the Seagram Building, the columns on the outside do provide the necessary support for the curtain wall but they're also purely symbolic. The use of the I-beam is both a decorative and a structural element.

JA: At what moment in the East River project does perception shift from awareness of the urban condition—the engineered river way, the architectural promenade—to noticing the vital detail of water current, barnacle crusting, tidal flux?

KS: There are ten marsh boxes. On a bridge next to them, designed by Kennedy & Violich, is a public walkway, and at both ends of the walkway is the seawall. When you're on the bridge, you're actually in and over the water, you see the water between the seawall and the bridge, so you are aware of the artificiality of the river environment that we've created in contemporary cities. But I think there is a sense of awe and wonder in being placed in a situation where you're over and surrounded by water and close up to a "primordial" marsh grass community—you can almost touch and smell the marsh and hear the gurgling of the bivalves. While it's not a true marsh, obviously, you do get a sense of the vegetation between you and the open water, and this starts to set up the kind of experience you would have in a natural situation. The notion of urban ecology is engaged by the contemporary condition of the water's edge. This experience is rooted in the pragmatics of the place and in what it takes to make this material structurally sound. The design accomplishes this in a symbolic way that speaks to the loss of the natural environment and creates a phenomenal experience.

Montage of final design

opposite:

Model of final design

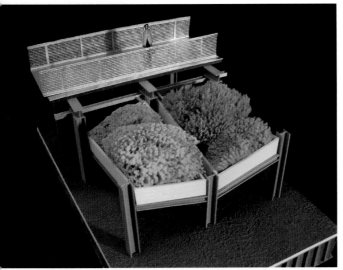

P.S. 19

Queens, New York

P.S. 19 is a pro-bono design project commissioned by the Robin Hood Foundation as part of the successful "Library Initiative," a program that engages leading architects to build libraries in the city's neediest neighborhoods. It is the first landscape project supported by the foundation. Ken Smith's schoolyard scheme offers a balance of pragmatism and pride, featuring low-cost, functional and kid-oriented solutions to typical conditions such as boundary definition, excessive asphalt paving, and the need for play space to be balanced with opportunities for outdoor learning. Five prototype elements were developed and then modified to address specific characteristics of the P.S. 19 site. In phase one, graphics were painted on the asphalt paving and on the walls of the "temporary" classrooms (now twenty years old). Later a cloud scrim was stretched across the schoolyard's chain link fence, raising the eye to an always-blue sky perimeter. A curtained space for reading was proposed, and modular seating made out of standard pipe segments was fabricated. The two elements most popular are the linear garden for butterflies

and birds and the movable mini dumpsters used for teaching and experimental plantings.

JA: **Now that your scheme for P.S. 19 has been in place for over two years, what bigger issues have emerged from this project to impact your other work?**

KS: P.S. 19 is the largest elementary school in New York City. In 2003 we completed the project—we had finished all design, collaborated with the fabricators and volunteer groups, installed the plantings, finished painting, and put up the cloud scrim. We had set up all elements of our design, but the big unknown was how the students and teachers would actually use the landscape. For example, we weren't sure how the learning gardens, a series of planted dumpsters, would develop into more than just something that was installed. There needed to be some mechanism that integrated the garden and its pieces into the school life. When I visited P.S. 19

Photographs of existing conditions at P.S. 19 and at Jackson
Boulevard (bottom)

opposite top and following spreads:
Five prototype elements were developed and modified to
address the specific characteristics of P.S. 19. Shown here
(opposite top) is the schoolyard fence prototype.

A graphic panel of sign material would be layered over the top portion of the tall school yard fence to create a strong image for the school and visually buffer the elevated train.

Product systems for this application include:
1. Printed Mesh Fabric, used for Times Square advertising
2. Reflective Paillettes, used for car wash signage

A garden of small plantings could be developed by filling common dumpsters like those used by the Board of Education with soil and plants.

The Dumpsters could be painted in graphic colors. Short dumpsters should be selected to reflect a child's height. A water faucet should be located nearby for maintenance.

Schoolyard plantings prototype

PVC drainage pipe commonly used in construction would be configured to create a diverse setting of modular and portable seating elements.

This lightweight and durable system of standard components include pipe sections, end caps and a variety of fittings and couplers ranging in sizes from 8" to 30" diameter.

WYE (Hub   **90° SHORT**   **VINYL TO**

22½° ELBOW   **45° ELBOW**   **45° STREET**

Schoolyard modular seating prototype

A graphic carpet could be created in the school yard using paint like that used by the D.O.T. The carpet could identify specific use areas or give an overall identity and sense of place to the whole site. Reflective glass beads like those used in city crosswalks could give sparkle and life to particular areas of the graphic pattern.

Paving and walls graphics prototype

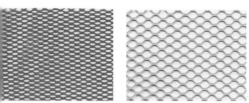

An outdoor curtain of construction netting would be used to enclose a reading space.

The transparency of the curtain material would create an area which is both spatially defined and visibly open. By moving the curtain the space could be transformed for differnect types of activity.

Place to read prototype

Modular seating mock-up

about two months ago, I discovered that the entire school had made the learning garden the focus of their studies for the spring semester. The art classes, the science classes—every teacher was doing things that involved the learning garden. It just blew me away. It made a big impact.

This project was really an essay for me, because in certain socially oriented schools and theories of public spaces, there is this sense that you can't have good design and social responsibility at the same time. It's the same kind of specious argument as saying you can't have good design and environmental responsiveness at the same time. P.S. 19 was my essay on how you can have social responsibility and community service within something that is a good design supported by a strong visual vocabulary.

JA: **Are there pieces of that strong visual vocabulary that are elbowing out additional program? The critic in me sees the polka dots as gratuitous; the kid in me sees prime territory.**

KS: I think everything is pretty well integrated. We'll know in a few more years if certain parts don't fit into the general scheme. For example, we've had some problems with the wind catching the cloud scrim. It has to be retied once or twice a year when we have especially strong winds. The scrim is inherently the most temporal part of the landscape because the material itself has only a shelf life of five years or so. It is commercially inkjet-printed and comes in big rolls, so it can easily be replicated and replaced. Whether or not the school will choose to do so I don't know. It's the most ephemeral piece in the design, the least enduring in some ways, but it was also the one that made the biggest splash in terms of totally readjusting the perception of the place. It's the element that will require the most commitment to replace. It's similar to the Japanese garden at Ise, where they rebuild the temple every twenty years. All public space involves a ritual of renewal. It's the ritual of sweeping the pavement or picking up the

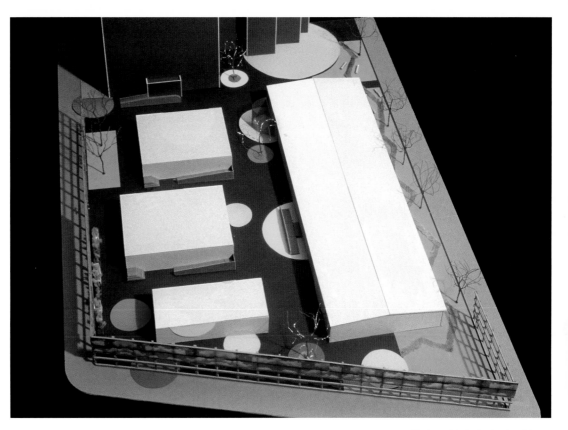

Study model of schoolyard prototypes

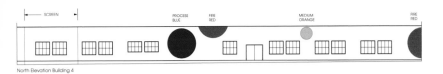

North Elevation Building 4

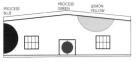

East Elevation Building 4

South Elevation Building 4

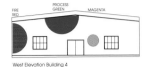

West Elevation Building 4

North Elevation Building 1

South Elevation Building 1

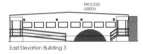

East Elevation Building 1

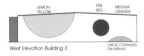

West Elevation Building 1

North Elevation Building 2

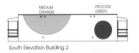

South Elevation Building 2

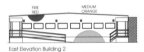

East Elevation Building 2

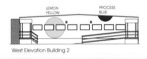

West Elevation Building 2

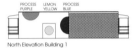

North Elevation Building 3

South Elevation Building 3

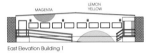

East Elevation Building 3

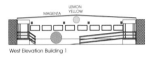

West Elevation Building 3

Schoolyard graphics, elevations

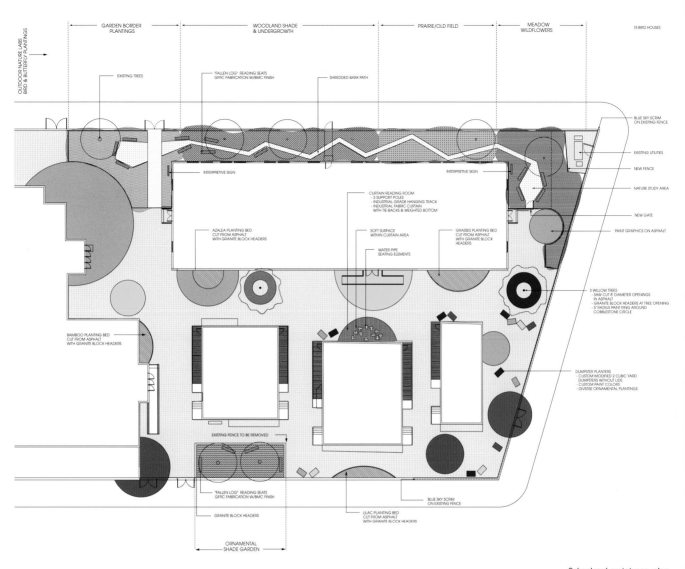

GARDEN BORDER
PLANTINGS

WOODLAND SHADE
& UNDERGROWTH

PRAIRIE/OLD FIELD

MEADOW
WILDFLOWERS

15 BIRD HOUSES

OUTDOOR NATURE LABS
BIRD & BUTTERFLY PLANTINGS

EXISTING TREES

"FALLEN LOG" READING SEATS
GFRC FABRICATION W/BMC FINISH

SHREDDED BARK PATH

BLUE SKY SCRIM
ON EXISTING FENCE

EXISTING UTILITIES

NEW FENCE

INTERPRETIVE SIGN

INTERPRETIVE SIGN

NATURE STUDY AREA

NEW GATE

CURTAIN READING ROOM
- 3 SUPPORT POLES
- INDUSTRIAL GRADE HANGING TRACK
- INDUSTRIAL FABRIC CURTAIN
  WITH TIE-BACKS & WEIGHTED BOTTOM

AZALEA PLANTING BED
CUT FROM ASPHALT
WITH GRANITE BLOCK HEADERS

SOFT SURFACE
WITHIN CURTAIN AREA

GRASSES PLANTING BED
CUT FROM ASPHALT
WITH GRANITE BLOCK
HEADERS

PAINT GRAPHICS ON ASPHALT

WATER PIPE
SEATING ELEMENTS

3 WILLOW TREES
- SAW CUT 8' DIAMETER OPENINGS
  IN ASPHALT
- GRANITE BLOCK HEADERS AT TREE OPENING
- 5' RADIUS PAINT RING AROUND
  COBBLESTONE CIRCLE

BAMBOO PLANTING BED
CUT FROM ASPHALT
WITH GRANITE BLOCK HEADERS

DUMPSTER PLANTERS
- CUSTOM MODIFIED 2 CUBIC YARD
  DUMPSTERS WITHOUT LIDS
- CUSTOM PAINT COLORS
- DIVERSE ORNAMENTAL PLANTINGS

EXISTING FENCE TO BE REMOVED

"FALLEN LOG" READING SEATS
GFRC FABRICATION W/BMC FINISH

BLUE SKY SCRIM
ON EXISTING FENCE

GRANITE BLOCK HEADERS

LILAC PLANTING BED
CUT FROM ASPHALT
WITH GRANITE BLOCK HEADERS

ORNAMENTAL
SHADE GARDEN

Schoolyard prototypes, plan

Placement of "blue sky" scrim, 2003

Schoolyard fence with "blue sky" scrim

The Bird and Butterfly Garden was planted with the help of volunteers on Earth Day in 2003.

Bird and Butterfly Garden, summer 2003

The dumpster planters were scaled down to a size comfortable for elemetary school students to plant and care for.

View of completed schoolyard from Jackson Boulevard

trash. Renewing the scrim has a longer temporal time frame than sweeping and a shorter one than rebuilding a temple, but essentially it's all the same ritual of continuity.

The teachers spray-painted numbers on the dumpsters, and each class signs up for one dumpster garden. There is a fair amount of competition between classes as the students adopt the gardens and take over the planting and weeding. In the summer the gardens are maintained by the New York Restoration Project, but eventually the school will take over.

When I reviewed the project a couple of months ago, I found a few bare spots in the bird and butterfly garden but most everything else did well. There were areas that needed to be replanted, and I realized that there was not enough of a winter bone structure. I had planted certain shrubs, including ilex and junipers, but it now became clear that there weren't quite enough. So I decided we needed to do a supplemental planting. I met with students who gave me a list of things they wanted to see in the garden. One student wanted roses so I've added roses, and somebody else wanted a bird bath. It's tough to design a garden for an academic calendar, which is, with its long break in the summer, exactly the opposite of when the plants want to grow.

This is a garden the kids see every day when they come to school. It's visible from the classrooms and from the street on three sides. There are certain areas where you actually pass through it—if you enter from the west side of the schoolyard you walk through it on your way to the school. And as part of the overall environment of the schoolyard, it's part of the students' daily life.

JA: **Has there been any vandalism?**

KS: No. There used to be a lot of vandalism at the school—graffiti mostly—and while I do believe that design can make a difference, I would never have

This photo was taken following completion of the schoolyard graphics in 2002.

promised the school that my garden would solve a graffiti or vandalism problem. But the building engineers and the superintendents have told me that there has been almost no vandalism or graffiti since the garden went in, which is just amazing. It's not just the students but also the parents who really love this garden. It's an important element of the community now, and communities have certain means of enforcing social norms. If something isn't acceptable within the community, people let each other know that.

Ken Smith, Landscape as Cultural Criticism

Nina Rappaport

In the work of Ken Smith, landscape architecture is a reinvigorated three-dimensional art form. Smith is devoted both to modern landscape aesthetics—as seen in projects by American landscape architects Dan Kiley (1912–2004), Paul Friedberg (b. 1931), and Robert Zion (b. 1921)—and to the expression of a contemporary urban place that engages the public through the artistic and inventive use of natural and artificial materials. From the modernists Smith learned how to articulate the differences between hardscapes and softscapes, to expose structure, to emphasize the contrast between urban forests and open spaces, and to formulate his idea of a sublime constructed nature that enhances urban experience. Smith also offers an ironic view of contemporary culture, imbuing his works with content in a subtle manipulation of form, material, and texture that encourages observers to perceive their environment in a new way.

For Smith the garden is first a place of separation, as experienced in walled villa gardens that remove people from the everyday. His creations are inspired by sixteenth-century Italian designers who manipulated space to form pleasure gardens—such as those at Tivoli's Villa d'Este—with faux lakes, miniature waterfalls, and perspective tricks to enhance the garden's scale. Inventing landscape is something that landscape architects have always done and have always been asked to do, and this often encourages an artistry that Smith expresses by trying to reveal both nature's nature and our nature in the world. He perceives gardens in fragmented contemporary cities as frames for communicating ideas that balance culture and nature, artifice and nature, and art and nature; every urban element is a kind of garden that offers an opportunity to reweave the city fabric. Smith's work at its most refined and thought-provoking has an irony to it, a critical edge that, as Linda Hutchinson notes of visual arts, is "a process of communication that entails two or more meanings being played off, one against the other. The irony is in

133

TOP AND OPPOSITE: Lever House, New York City,
landscape restoration, 1999–2002

the difference; irony makes the difference. It plays between meanings, in a space that is always affectively charged, that always has a critical edge."[1]

This play is seen in Smith's juxtaposition of unconventional garden materials, reuse of everyday objects, and transformations of one form into another. The design for MoMA's camouflage roof garden is an example of this commentary; Smith's rooftop installation raises questions about what is real in an urban garden made of artificial materials such as plastic trees and glass shards, a faux-scape that is colorful year-round and visible only to residents of the adjacent high-rise. The garden is a camouflage both of the building and of nature—there is no real nature, and the flat roof now has a décor. The uninhabitable roofscape is for display only, not for physical experience; it is similar to looking at a painting on a wall. From a distance one cannot even discern what kind of materials are used; one sees only relatively inert color, pattern, and form.

Smith's approach is characterized by its complementary natures: it is both the approach of a creative artist who has a varied palette and that of a pragmatic craftsman. This pragmatism and his indicative love for truthful detail allow Smith to determine how everyday materials and their performance can be employed to reveal the content behind the landscape in the making. Not that the nuts and bolts are shown, but the way the pieces are put together is demystified and visible (although other cerebral games may be being played).

For Smith client and program parameters are part of the design challenge and the puzzle that his work has to fit within. His work is a strategic expression of his preoccupation with the public agencies or clients for whom he is designing. For the renovation of the Lever House Plaza in New York, Smith researched the original schemes in the Noguchi archives and, with landscape architect Gavin Keeney, recreated the original

design concepts while upgrading the plaza for contemporary needs. In the improvement project for Lawrence Halprin's dilapidated Manhattan Square Park (1974) in Rochester, New York, the work was phased so that the disused areas of the fountain and the stage can be revitalized, while the remainder of the park is only minimally redesigned until the city obtains further funding.

At the same time, as an artist, Smith reinvigorates landscape architecture as a conceptual art form, imbuing it with allusions to culture. Drawing a parallel between fashion as a cultural phenomenon and landscape architecture, he says both are "artificial constructions that fit an organic body that moves and fluctuates....It is an ideological expression, making or revealing the body, or in the case of landscape—the city." Smith notes that fashion was seen as a regressive art form until critics such as Richard Martin evaluated it as a form of cultural expression, and he feels that this is how the public views landscape design as well. Many of

Smith's projects begin as temporary installations. Often made of disposable materials, they give him the freedom to experiment and investigate more complex ideas for future permanent structures. The temporary nature of these designs emphasizes the weighty element of time in landscape architecture, in relation to both natural and artificial materials. While the artificial elements in Smith's works can be removed, they do not die or change quickly. This allows the designer more control over the palette. In contrast, the natural landscape is predictable but not stable. It is rendered temporary by its constant process of change while the artificial landscape is temporary because it is disposable. For example, the synthetic materials of the MoMA roof garden need only last the life of the roof contractor's guarantee.

Although Smith does not promote environmentalism per se, he is an environmentalist in subtle ways while not making a moral distinction of it. For him the environment is something to be respected and understood as a given. For the East River Ferry Landings, for example, Smith selected natural grasses to be planted in floating containers—hinting at what was once there as well as at what could be if there was no retaining wall at the river's edge.

Smith's design approach reintegrates often obscure and fragmented sites into the public realm in celebratory ways as he transforms them into something beyond the norm. His conceptual strategies adapt to the local conditions and specific sites in an inductive method by first appreciating what is there. His artistic and inventive yet practical approach, environmental sensitivity, and broad artificial and natural material palette, intertwine to make spaces that transform daily life and engage the public.

1 Linda Hutchinson, *Irony's Edge* (London and New York: Routledge, 1994), 105.

Credits

The projects in this monograph result from a team effort in my office. I'd like to especially thank Elizabeth Asawa, Senior Associate, who has been involved in all of these works and plays an important role in the operation of the office. The project managers played a significant role in the design of each project: Alex Felson for the East River Ferry Landings, Annie Weinmayr for P.S. 19, and Tobias Armborst and Matt Landis for the MoMA Roof Garden.

Ken Smith

The Museum of Modern Art Roof Garden

CLIENT
The Museum of Modern Art

LANDSCAPE ARCHITECT
Ken Smith Landscape Architect

DESIGN TEAM
Tobias Armborst
Elizabeth Asawa
David Hamerman
Matt Landis
Rocio Lastras
Ken Smith
Annie Weinmayr
Judith Wong
Christian Zimmermann

LANDSCAPE CONTRACTOR
Town and Gardens

East River Ferrry Landings

CLIENT
New York City Economic Development Corporation
New York City Department of Transportation
New York City Department of Parks and Recreation

LANDSCAPE ARCHITECT
Ken Smith Landscape Architect

DESIGN TEAM
Tobias Armborst
Elizabeth Asawa
Heike Bergdolt
Yoonchul Cho
Alex Felson
Ruth Hartmann
Rocio Lastras Montana
Ken Smith
Dan Willner

ARCHITECT
Kennedy & Violich Architecture

MARINE/STRUCTURAL ENGINEERS
M. G. McLaren, P.C.

CONSTRUCTION MANAGERS
Hudson Meridian Construction Group

M/E/P
Lakhani & Jordan Engineering

SECURITY
Cosentini Associates

P.S. 19

CLIENT
Robin Hood Foundation

OWNER
New York City Department of
Education, P.S.19 (Genie Calibar,
current principal, Cathy Zarbis,
former principal)

LANDSCAPE ARCHITECT
Ken Smith Landscape Architect

DESIGN TEAM
Tobias Armborst
Elizabeth Asawa
Alex Felson
Alice Mahin
Ken Smith
Annie Weinmayr
Judith Wong

CONTRACTOR
The New York Restoration Project

GRAPHIC DESIGN
Pentagram

NURSERY
Bissett Nursery Corporation

RECLAIMED LOG SUPPLIER
CitiLog

DUMPSTER MANUFACTURER
J. C. Industries

**DAFFODIL PROJECT
COORDINATION**
New Yorkers for Parks/The Urban
Center

ADDITIONAL CONTRIBUTORS
The Audubon Society
Clear Channel/Spectacolor
Danielle and David Ganek
Maureen Gibbons
Mimi and Peter Haas
Overbrook Foundation
Peter Peterson
SignCraft
Timberland Corporation

IMAGE CREDITS
All images are by Ken Smith
Landscape Architect unless
otherwise noted.
Pages 11 left (top and bottom),
    12 left, 41, 42 (left), 79 bottom,
    82, 91 (bottom), 101: © Daniel
    Willner
Pages 11 middle (top and
    bottom), 21 (bottom), 26, 43,
    44, 52, 53, 55–65, 134, 135:
    © Peter Mauss/Esto
Pages 13 left (top and bottom),
    92, 117, 126-127, 129: © Albert
    Večerka/Esto
Pages 13 right (top and bottom),
    111, 115, 118-119, 121-123, 125,
    130-131: © Paul Warchol
Pages 14, 21: © Nathaniel
    Goldberg
Page 21 (top): © Betsy Pinover
    Schiff
Page 23 (right): © John Bach

Bibliography

Peter Reed, *Groundswell, Constructing the Contemporary Landscape*. New York: The Museum of Modern Art, 2005.

Barbara Hoffman, "It's Art-ificial." *New York Post*, 21 February 2005.

Allen Freeman, "Big Dots, Little Dumpsters." *Landscape Architecture Magazine* (February 2005).

Kenneth Helphand "Hortus Ludens." *Landscape Architecture Magazine* (February 2005).

Allen Freeman, "Proving Ground." *Landscape Architecture Magazine* (January 2005).

Charles Birnbaum, ed. *Preserving Modern Landscape Architecture II, Making Postwar Landscapes Visible*. Washington, D.C.: Spacemaker Press, 2004.

Ann Raver, "A Roof Top Garden With Synthetic Green." *The New York Times*, 11 November 2004.

Toby Musgrave, "Out of the Blue." *Gardens Illustrated* (October 2004).

Ken Smith, "Railyard Park, Santa Fe, New Mexico." *Dialogue: Architecture+Design+Culture, Taiwan*. Special Issue on Landscape Architecture (September 2003).

Karen E. Steen, "Garden Spot." *Metropolis Magazine* (August/September 2004).

Deborah Bishop, "Landscape Architecture 101—Aluminum Garden." *Dwell Magazine* (July/August 2004).

Ken Smith, West 8, Field Operations, D.I.R.T. Studio, "Why Not A Park." *The New York Times Magazine*, Architecture 2004 (May 16, 2004).

Laura Starr, "Ayalon Park—Extreme Sites: The Greening of the Brownfield." *AD Magazine* (March/April 2004).

David Coleman, "Out in the Garden, a Reputation Blooms." *The New York Times*, 11 July 2003.

Sharon McHugh, "New Life for a Troubled Plaza." *Competitions Magazine* Vol. 132, No. 2 (Summer 2003).

Debra Gibson, "LA Alumnus a Force Majeure in Design Circles." *Design News*, Iowa State University (Spring 2003).

Carrie Geyer, "Stop and Smell the Dumpsters." *The Lantern*, Ohio State University (23 May 2003).

Leslie Sherr, "Manhattan Takeover," Lever House. *I.D. The International Design Magazine* (April 2003).

Suzanne Stephens, "Projects: Lever House." *Architectural Record* (March 2003).

Suzanne Stephens, "Commentary: Collaborations at the WTC." *Architectural Record* (March 2003).

Kim Sorvig, "Competing for Santa Fe's Identity." *Landscape Architecture Magazine* (March 2003).

Anne Raver, "This Stop: 68th Floor, Rain Forest." *The New York Times*, 13 February 2003.

Lisa Speckhardt, "Riverfront Revival." *Landscape Architecture Magazine* (January 2003).

Ruth La Ferla, "Let Me Guess, You Must Be an Architect." *The New York Times*, 9 February 2003.

Herbert Muschamp, "Balancing Reason and Emotion in Trade Towers Void." *The New York Times*, 6 February 2003.

Herbert Muschamp, "A Goal for Ground Zero: Finding an Urban Poetry." *The New York Times*, 28 January 2003.

Cherilyn "Liv" Wright, "A Visual Explosion in Harlem." *The International Review of African American Art*, 2002.

Patrick Frank, "Environmental Design." *Artforms, An Introduction to the Visual Arts*. Upper Saddle River, NJ: Prentice Hall, 2002.

Anne Raver, "The Places He'll Go To Green the City." *The New York Times*, 14 November 2002.

Kim Sorvig, "Railyard Remake in Santa Fe." *Competitions Magazine* Vol.12, No. 3 (Fall 2002).

David Dunlap, "Plan Chosen for Redesign of a Plaza at 55 Water Street." *The New York Times*, 21 September 2002.

Edward Wyatt, "Design Teams are Selected for New Plans for 9/11 Site." *The New York Times*, 27 September 2002.

Lisa Rochon, "Up from the Ashes." *The Globe and Mail*, Canada, 10 April 2002.

Zoe Ryan, "Dumpster Gardens, Designing Queens Plaza." *Van Alen Report* #11 (January 2001).

Jane Amidon, *Radical Landscapes*. London: Thames and Hudson, 2001.

James Grayson Trulove, "Retreat Pool." *The New American Swimming Pool*. Connecticut: Whitney Press, 2001.

"Debate Over World Trade Center Memorial." *CBS Evening News*, 11 December 2001.

Terence Riley, et al., "What to Build." *The New York Times Magazine*, 11 November 2001.

Stephanie Cash, "Noguchi Garden for Lever House." *Art In America* (March 2001).

Ken Smith, "What New York Needs Now." *The Architectural League of New York* (Spring/Summer 2001).

Marc Kristal, "Think It Yourself." *Dwell Magazine* (June 2001).

Melissa Davis, "Sleek Modernity." *Garden Design Magazine* (May 2001).

Lisa Speckhardt, "In The Public Eye." *Landscape Architecture Magazine*, May 2001.

Danielle Reed, "Gardening on the Cheap." *Wall Street Journal*, 27 April 2001.

Ken Smith, "Aluminum Garden." *Pages Paysages* No. 8 (January 2001).

David Colman, "10 to Watch, The Design World in 2001." *House & Garden Magazine* (January 2001).

Gavin Keeney, "Idiosyncratic Public Open Space." *On The Nature Of Things, Contemporary American Landscape Architecture*, Basel: Birkhauser, 2000.

James Grayson Trulove, "Aluminum Garden." *Pocket Gardens, Big Ideas for Small Spaces*. New York: Morrow Press, 2000.

David Colman, "Garden Goes Pop, Garden Daisies." *Garden Design Magazine* (October 2000).

Ken Smith and Alice Adams, "A Long Look at Fifth Avenue, DLF II: Unbuilt Landscapes." *Land Forum* 06 (2000).

"New York Plaza." *Van Alen Report* #8 (Fall 2000).

"Gateway to Harlem, Neighborhood Revitalizations Establish a Sense of Place and Memorialize Malcolm X." *Landscape Architecture Magazine* (November 2000).

Joseph Holtzman, "Question of Decency."*Every Room Tells A Story*, *Nest Magazine* 9 (Summer 2000)

Gavin Keeney, "A Paradisical New Plaza." *Oculus Magazine* (Summer 2000).

Ann Raver, "A Sliver of Paradise Blooms in Harlem." *The New York Times*, 3 August 2000.

Elaine Louie, "Aluminum is Getting Hot." *The New York Times*, 6 July 2000.

Tobias Schneebaum, "Hotel Eden." *Nest Magazine* (Summer 2000).

Gina Crandell, "Glowing Topiary Winter Garden." *Land Forum* 04 (2000).

Ken Smith, "Case Study: Preserving Dan Kiley's Work at Lincoln Center for the Performing

Arts." *Preserving Modern Landscape Architecture, Proceedings of the Wave Hill Conference*. Washington, D.C.: Spacemaker Press, 1999.

Mary Jane Pool and Betsy Pinover Schiff, "Gardens of Light." *Gardens in the City, New York in Bloom*. New York: Abrams Press, 1999.

Nils Ballhausen, "Urban Landscapes." *Bauwelt* (October 1999).

Ken Smith, "Linear Landscapes." *Harvard Design Magazine* (Spring 1999).

Catherine Slessor, "Delights." *The Architectural Review*, London (December 1998).

Elaine Louie, "Where Mies Could Towel Off." *The New York Times*, 3 September 1998.

Elaine Louie, "The Art of the Hirsute." *The New York Times*, 6 August 1998.

Koji Aikawa, "Linkages with Urban Activity." *Space Design Magazine*, Landscape Creation Today: The Challenges of Landscape Architects Issue (June 1998).

Paul Bennett, "On the Boards, Reinventing Harlem." *Landscape Architecture Magazine* (June 1998).

David Simon Morton, "Animated and Interactive Design Lights Up Financial District." *Architectural Record*, AIA Honor Awards Issue (May 1998).

Wanda Jankowski, "Garden Variety." *Architectural Lighting Magazine* (April–May 1998).

Francisco Asensio Cerver, "Village of Yorkville Park." *Landscape Architecture 02, The World of*

Environmental Design Atrium International, Spain (1997).

Gina Crandell and Heidi Landecker, ed., "Parks." *Designed Landscape Forum.* Washington, D.C.: Spacemaker Press, 1997.

Elaine Louie, "Currents." Glowing Topiary Garden Project, *The New York Times,* 7 December 1997 and front page photo, *The New York Times,* 17 December 1997.

Elaine Louie, "Currents." Fifth Avenue Chandeliers Project, *The New York Times,* 3 July 1997.

Ken Smith, "Preserving a Modernist Legacy." *Harvard University GSD News* (Fall 1996).

Anne Elizabeth Powell, "Northern Exposure, President's Award of Excellence." Village of Yorkville Park, *Landscape Architecture Magazine* (November 1996).

Nina Rappaport, "On The Drawing Boards." *Oculus Magazine* (June 1996).

"Yorkville Residents Roam Canadian Landscape—In an Urban Park." *Architectural Record* (July 1995).

Roberta Brandes Gratz, "Filling the Void in Public Works." *Progressive Architecture Magazine* (March 1995).

George Thomas Kapelos, *Interpretations of Nature, Contemporary Canadian Architecture, Landscape and Urbanism,* Kleinburg, ON:McMichael Canadian Art Collection, 1994.

"Excavating The Commonplace, Visionary Landscapes." *Landscape Architecture Magazine* (December 1994).

Rick Andrighetti, "Facing the Land, Yorkville Park." *The Canadian Architect* (August 1994).

Ken Smith, "Relics, Prosthetics and Surrogate Realities." The Culture of Landscape Architecture, Australia, 1994.

Eve Kahn, "News, Controversial Toronto Parks." *Landscape Architecture Magazine* (July 1994).

Jean Godfrey-June, "Personalities: Rocking Toronto." *Contract Design* magazine, December 1993.

J. William Thompson, "Drawing, Portfolios." *Landscape Architecture Magazine* (May 1993).

Mac Griswald, "Box Set: Cumberland Park." Parks Beyond Olmsted Issue, *Landscape Architecture Magazine* (April 1993).

Ken Smith, "Computer Space In The Design Of Landscape." *Canadian Society of Decorative Arts Bulletin* (Autumn 1992).

"Urban Renewal Project." *Metropolis* (October 1992).

Gary Strang, "Landscape Architecture, The Expanding Scope and Evolving Roles," University of California, Davis, Video, 1992.

"News, Cumberland Park Competition Winner Announced." *Landscape Architecture Magazine* (February 1992).

"News, Brooklyn Bridge Garden Mount" *Landscape Architecture Magazine* (January 1991).

Michael Leccese and J. William Thompson, "Landscapes for the 21st Century." *Landscape Architecture Magazine* (December 1990).

Biographies

JANE AMIDON is a landscape designer, critic, and lecturer currently teaching in the Landscape Section of the Knowlton School of Architecture. Her published work includes *Dan Kiley: America's Master Landscape Architect*, *Radical Landscapes*, and *Moving Horizons: The Landscape Architecture of Kathryn Gustafson and Partners*. Recent presentations include discussions of modern and contemporary landscape architecture at the Netherlands Architecture Institute, the Royal Institute of British Architecture, and the Wexner Art Center.

NINA RAPPAPORT is an architectural critic, curator, and educator based in New York. She is publications editor at Yale School of Architecture where she is the editor of the biannual publication *Constructs*, exhibition catalogs, and studio books. She is a fellow of the Design Trust for Public Space for "Long Island City, Connecting the Arts," an arts identity and urban design project. She has contributed articles to *Architecture, Architectural Record, Deutsche Bauzeitung, Future Anterior, Metropolis, Praxis*, and *Tec21*. At City College she is adjunct professor, teaching seminars on the post-industrial factory and on innovative engineers. She is co-chair of the New York/Tri-state chapter of Docomomo/US.